The Con

# Cancer Diet &
# Nutrition Therapy

Nutritious Anti-Cancer
Diet Recipes Cookbook
for the Newly Diagnosed

Serena Kafta

# THE COMPLETE
# CANCER DIET &
# NUTRITION THERAPY

Nutritious Anti-Cancer Diet Recipes Cookbook for the Newly Diagnosed

## Serena Kafta

# Copyright Page

All rights reserved. No part of this publication may be reproduced, distributed, or transmitted in any form or by any means, including photocopying, recording, or other electronic or mechanical methods, without the publisher's prior written permission.

Copyright © 2022 by Serena Kafta

# Table of Contents

# Introduction

Cancer isn't a single disease. Cancer is a group of diseases characterized by the uncontrolled proliferation of cells. Ignoring the body's signal to stop, malignant cells multiply to form tumors in organs and tissues or, in the case of blood cancers, crowd out normal cells in the blood stream and bone marrow.

In a healthy body, cells grow and divide in a controlled, orderly fashion to replace those that have grown old or have been damaged and die by design in a process called apoptosis. Cancer occurs when these natural processes go awry.

When the genetic material of a cell- the DNA- is damaged, mutations can arise, potentially disrupting normal growth and division. An accumulation of mutations can turn normal cells into precancerous cells, which sometimes multiply and evolve into cancer cells. Cancer is a result of the accumulation of these cells.

Cancer is not an event, but a process that takes time, often years, to develop. The length of time varies widely and depends on the identity, order, and speed at which mutations accumulate.

The stage of cancer describes the progression of the disease in the body from precancer to cancer that has spread to distant organs or tissue–metastatic cancer.

Cancer spreads through the body via a process called metastasis. Cancer cells break away from their original location, travel through the blood or the lymph system, and form new tumors in other parts of the body. Cancer metastases are most commonly found in the bones, liver, or lungs.

Our body is made up of billions of cells. Normal healthy cells grow and multiply in an orderly, controlled manner. Cancer cells, on the other hand, multiply uncontrollably. They do not function normally and instead form a growth or tumour. These cancerous tumours can spread to nearby tissues and organs as well as to other parts of the body. Cancer kills by:

- Destroying important organs
- Disturbing normal bodily functions
- Blocking important blood vessels or air passages

About one quarter of all deaths are caused by cancer. Cancer can be detected early and may be prevented, and you can help to keep yourself at low risk. Find out how you can protect yourself or reduce the risk of cancer.

## What is cancer?

Cancer is a condition where cells in a specific part of the body grow and reproduce uncontrollably. The cancerous cells can invade and destroy surrounding healthy tissue, including organs.

Cancer sometimes begins in one part of the body before spreading to other areas. This process is known as metastasis. You can find out more about specific types of cancer by using the links on this page.

## Spotting signs of cancer

Changes to your body's normal processes or symptoms that are out of the ordinary can sometimes be an early sign of cancer.

For example, a lump that suddenly appears on your body, unexplained bleeding or changes to your bowel habits are all symptoms that need to be checked by a doctor.

In many cases, your symptoms will not be related to cancer and will be caused by other, non-cancerous health conditions. However, it is still important that you see your doctor so your symptoms can be investigated.

## Cancer symptoms

It is important to be aware of any unexplained changes to your body, such as the sudden appearance of a lump, blood in your urine or a change in your usual bowel habits.

These symptoms are often caused by other, non-cancerous illnesses, but it is important you see your doctor so they can investigate.

Other potential signs and symptoms of cancer are outlined below.

**Lump in your breast**

See your doctor if you notice a lump in your breast, or if you have a lump that is rapidly increasing in size elsewhere on your body.

Your doctor will refer you to a specialist for tests if they think you may have cancer.

**Coughing, chest pain and breathlessness**

You should visit your doctor if you have had a cough for more than three weeks.

Symptoms such as shortness of breath or chest pain may be a sign of an acute (severe) condition, such as pneumonia (a lung infection). Go to see your doctor straight away if you experience these types of symptoms.

**Changes in bowel habits**

Go to see your doctor if you have experienced one of the changes listed below and it has lasted for more than a few weeks:

- blood in your stools
- diarrhoea or constipation for no obvious reason

- a feeling of not having fully emptied your bowels after going to the toilet
- pain in your abdomen (tummy) or your anus (back passage)
- persistent bloating

**Bleeding**

You should also go to see your doctor if you have any unexplained bleeding such as:

- blood in your urine
- bleeding between periods
- blood from your back passage
- blood when you cough
- blood in your vomit

**Moles**

Go to see your doctor if you have a mole that:

- has an irregular or asymmetrical shape
- has an irregular border with jagged edges
- has more than one colour (it may be flecked with brown, black, red, pink or white)
- is bigger then 7mm in diameter
- is itchy, crusting or bleeding

Any of the above changes means that there is a chance you have malignant melanoma (skin cancer).

**Unexplained weight loss**

You should also go to see your doctor if you have lost a lot of weight over the last couple of months that cannot be explained by changes to your diet, exercise or stress.

**Reducing your risk of cancer**

Making some simple changes to your lifestyle can significantly reduce your risk of developing cancer. For example, healthy eating, taking regular exercise) and not smoking will all help lower your risk.

**How common is cancer?**

Cancer is a common condition.

The most common types of cancer are:

- breast cancer
- prostate cancer

- lung cancer
- bowel cancer
- bladder cancer
- uterine (womb) cancer

## Breast cancer in women

Breast cancer is the most common type of cancer in the UK. Most women diagnosed with breast cancer are over 50, but younger women can also get breast cancer.

About one in eight women are diagnosed with breast cancer during their lifetime. There's a good chance of recovery if it's detected in its early stages.

For this reason, it's vital that women check their breasts regularly for any changes and always get any changes examined by their doctor.

## Symptoms of breast cancer

Breast cancer can have a number of symptoms, but the first noticeable symptom is usually a lump or area of thickened breast tissue.

Most breast lumps aren't cancerous, but it's always best to have them checked by your doctor.

You should also see your doctor if you notice any of the following:

- a change in the size or shape of one or both breasts
- discharge from either of your nipples, which may be streaked with blood
- a lump or swelling in either of your armpits
- dimpling on the skin of your breasts
- a rash on or around your nipple

- a change in the appearance of your nipple, such as becoming sunken into your breast

Breast pain is not a symptom of breast cancer.

## Causes of breast Cancer

The causes of breast cancer aren't fully understood, making it difficult to say why one woman may develop breast cancer and another may not.

However, there are risk factors known to affect your likelihood of developing breast cancer. Some of these you can't do anything about, but there are some you can change.

## Age

The risk of developing breast cancer increases with age. The condition is most common among women over 50 who have been through the menopause. About 8 out of 10 cases of breast cancer occur in women over 50.

All women who are 50 to 70 years of age should be screened for breast cancer every three years as part of the NHS Breast Screening Programme. Women over the age of 70 are still eligible to be screened and can arrange this through their doctor or local screening unit.

**Family history**

If you have close relatives who have had breast cancer or ovarian cancer, you may have a higher risk of developing breast cancer.

However, because breast cancer is the most common cancer in women, it's possible for it to occur in more than one family member by chance.

Most cases of breast cancer don't run in families, but particular genes known as BRCA1 and BRCA2 can increase your risk of developing both breast and ovarian cancer. It's possible for these genes to be passed on from a parent to their child.

Other newly detected genes, such as TP53 and CHEK 2, are also associated with an increased risk of breast cancer.

If you have, for example, two or more close relatives from the same side of your family such as your mother, sister or daughter – who have had breast cancer under the age of 50, you may be eligible for surveillance for breast cancer, or genetic screening to look for the genes that make developing breast cancer more likely.

If you're worried about your family history of breast cancer, discuss it with your doctor.

Other causes include:

- a previous diagnosis of breast cancer
- a previous benign breast lump
- being tall, overweight or obese
- excessive use of alcohol

## Diagnosing breast cancer

After examining your breasts, your doctor may refer you to a specialist breast cancer clinic for further tests. This might include breast screening (mammography) or a biopsy.

## Types of breast cancer

There are several different types of breast cancer, which can develop in different parts of the breast.

Breast cancer is often divided into:

- non-invasive breast cancer (carcinoma in situ) – found in the ducts of the breast (ductal carcinoma in situ, DCIS) and hasn't developed the ability to spread outside the breast. It's usually found during a mammogram and rarely shows as a breast lump.
- invasive breast cancer – usually develops in the cells that line the breast ducts (invasive ductal breast cancer) and is the most common type of breast cancer. It can spread outside the breast, although this doesn't necessarily mean it has spread.

Other less common types of breast cancer include:

- invasive (and pre-invasive) lobular breast cancer
- inflammatory breast cancer

## Breast cancer screening

Mammographic screening, where X-ray images of the breast are taken, is the most commonly available method of detecting an early breast lesion.

However, you should be aware that a mammogram might fail to detect some breast cancers.

It might also increase your chances of having extra tests and interventions, including surgery, even if you're not affected by breast cancer. Women with a higher-than-average risk of developing breast cancer may be offered screening and genetic testing for the condition.

## Treating breast cancer

If cancer is detected at an early stage, it can be treated before it spreads to nearby parts of the body.

Breast cancer is treated using a combination of:

- surgery
- chemotherapy
- radiotherapy

Surgery is usually the first type of treatment you'll have, followed by chemotherapy or radiotherapy or, in some cases, hormone or biological treatments.

The type of surgery and the treatment you have afterwards will depend on the type of breast cancer you have. Your doctor will discuss the best treatment plan with you.

In a small proportion of women, breast cancer is discovered after it is spread to other parts of the body (metastatic breast cancer).

Secondary cancer, also called advanced or metastatic cancer, is not curable, so the aim of treatment is to achieve remission (symptom relief).

## Living with breast cancer

Being diagnosed with breast cancer can affect daily life in many ways, depending on what stage it's at and the treatment you're having.

How women cope with their diagnosis and treatment varies from person to person. You can be reassured that there are several forms of support available, if you need it.

For example:

- your family and friends can be a powerful support system
- you can communicate with other people in the same situation
- find out as much as possible about your condition
- don't try to do too much or overexert yourself
- make time for yourself

## Preventing breast cancer

As the causes of breast cancer aren't fully understood, at the moment it's not possible to know if it can be prevented.

If you're at increased risk of developing the condition, some treatments are available to reduce the risk.

Studies have looked at the link between breast cancer and diet. Although there are no definite conclusions, there are benefits for women who:

- maintain a healthy weight
- exercise regularly
- have a low intake of saturated fat and alcohol

It's been suggested that regular exercise can reduce your risk of breast cancer by as much as a third. Regular exercise and a healthy lifestyle can also improve the outlook for people affected by breast cancer. If you've been through the menopause, it is particularly important that you're not overweight or obese.

This is because being overweight or obese causes more oestrogen to be produced, which can increase the risk of breast cancer.

## Prostate cancer

Prostate cancer is the most common cancer in men in the UK, with over 40,000 new cases diagnosed every year.

Prostate cancer usually develops slowly, so there may be no signs you have it for many years.

Symptoms often only become apparent when your prostate is large enough to affect the urethra (the tube that carries urine from the bladder to the penis).

When this happens, you may notice things like an increased need to urinate, straining while urinating and a feeling that your bladder has not fully emptied.

These symptoms should not be ignored, but they do not mean you definitely have prostate cancer. It is more likely that they are caused by something else, such as benign prostatic hyperplasia (also known as BPH or prostate enlargement).

## Tests for prostate cancer

There is no single test for prostate cancer. All the tests used to help diagnose the condition have benefits and risks, which your doctor should discuss with you.

The most commonly used tests for prostate cancer are blood tests , a physical examination of your prostate (known as a digital rectal examination or DRE ) and a biopsy .

The blood test, known as a prostate-specific antigen (PSA) test, measures the level of PSA and may help detect early prostate cancer. Men are not routinely offered PSA tests to screen for prostate cancer, as results can be unreliable.

This is because the PSA blood test is not specific to prostate cancer. PSA can be raised due to a large non-cancerous growth of the prostate (BPH), a urinary tract infection or inflammation of the prostate, as well as prostate cancer.

Raised PSA levels also cannot tell a doctor whether a man has life-threatening prostate cancer or not. This means a raised PSA can lead to unnecessary tests and treatment.

However, you can ask to be tested for prostate cancer once the benefits and risks have been explained to you.

## How is prostate cancer treated?

For many men with prostate cancer, treatment is not immediately necessary.

If the cancer is at an early stage and not causing symptoms, a policy of "watchful waiting" or "active surveillance" may be adopted. This involves carefully monitoring your condition.

Some cases of prostate cancer can be cured if treated in the early stages. Treatments include surgically removing the prostate, radiotherapyand hormone therapy.

Some cases are only diagnosed at a later stage when the cancer has spread. If the cancer spreads to other parts of the body, typically the bones, it cannot be cured and treatment is focused on prolonging life and relieving symptoms.

All treatment options carry the risk of significant side effects, including erectile dysfunction and urinary incontinence . For this reason, many men choose to delay treatment until there is a risk the cancer might spread.

Newer treatments, such as high-intensity focused ultrasound (HIFU) or cryotherapy, aim to reduce these side effects. Some hospitals may offer them as an alternative to surgery, radiotherapy or hormone therapy. However, the long-term effectiveness of these treatments are not yet known.

## Living with prostate cancer

As prostate cancer usually progresses very slowly, you can live for decades without symptoms or needing treatment.

Nevertheless, it can have an effect on your life. As well as causing physical problems such as erectile dysfunction and urinary incontinence , a diagnosis of prostate cancer can understandably make you feel anxious or depressed .

You may find it beneficial to talk about the condition with your family, friends, a family doctor and other men with prostate cancer.

Financial support is also available if prostate cancer reduces your ability to work.

## Symptoms of prostate cancer

Prostate cancer does not normally cause symptoms until the cancer has grown large enough to put pressure on the urethra.

This normally results in problems associated with urination. Symptoms can include:

- needing to urinate more frequently, often during the night
- needing to rush to the toilet
- difficulty in starting to pee (hesitancy)
- straining or taking a long time while urinating
- weak flow
- feeling that your bladder has not emptied fully

Many men's prostates get larger as they get older due to a non-cancerous condition known as prostate enlargement or benign prostatic hyperplasia.

Symptoms that the cancer may have spread include bone and back pain, a loss of appetite, pain in the testicles and unexplained weight loss.

## Causes of prostate cancer

It is not known exactly what causes prostate cancer, although a number of things can increase your risk of developing the condition.

These include:

- Age – risk rises as you get older and most cases are diagnosed in men over 50 years of age.

- Ethnic group – prostate cancer is more common among men of African-Caribbean and African descent than in men of Asian descent.

- Family history – having a brother or father who developed prostate cancer under the age of 60 seems to increase the risk of you developing it. Research also shows that having a close female relative who developed breast cancer may also increase your risk of developing prostate cancer.

- Obesity – recent research suggests that there may be a link between obesity and prostate cancer.

- Exercise – men who regularly exercise have also been found to be at lower risk of developing prostate cancer.

- Diet – research is ongoing into the links between diet and prostate cancer. There is evidence that a diet high in calcium is linked to an increased risk of developing prostate cancer.

In addition, some research has shown that prostate cancer rates appear to be lower in men who eat foods containing certain nutrients including lycopene, found in cooked tomatoes and other red fruit, and selenium, found in brazil nuts. However, more research is needed.

## Lung cancer

Lung cancer is one of the most common and serious types of cancer. Around 44,500 people are diagnosed with the condition every year in the UK.

There are usually no signs or symptoms in the early stages of lung cancer, but many people with the condition eventually develop symptoms including:

- a persistent cough
- coughing up blood
- persistent breathlessness
- unexplained tiredness and weight loss
- an ache or pain when breathing or coughing

You should see your doctor if you have these symptoms.

## Types of lungs cancer

Cancer that begins in the lungs is called primary lung cancer. Cancer that spreads to the lungs from another place in the body is known as secondary lung cancer. This page is about primary lung cancer.

There are two main types of primary lung cancer. These are classified by the type of cells in which the cancer starts. They are:

- non-small-cell lung cancer – the most common type, accounting for more than 80% of cases; can be either squamous cell carcinoma, adenocarcinoma or large-cell carcinoma
- small-cell lung cancer – a less common type that usually spreads faster than non-small-cell lung cancer

The type of lung cancer you have determines which treatments are recommended.

**Who's affected**

Lung cancer mainly affects older people. It's rare in people younger than 40, and the rates of lung cancer rise sharply with age. Lung cancer is most commonly diagnosed in people aged 70-74.

Although people who have never smoked can develop lung cancer, smoking is the main cause (accounting for over 85% of cases). This is because smoking involves regularly inhaling a number of different toxic substances.

## Treating lung cancer

Treatment depends on the type of cancer, how far it's spread and how good your general health is.

If the condition is diagnosed early and the cancerous cells are confined to a small area, surgery to remove the affected area of lung is usually recommended.

If surgery is unsuitable due to your general health, radiotherapy to destroy the cancerous cells may be recommended instead.

If the cancer has spread too far for surgery or radiotherapy to be effective, chemotherapy is usually used.

## Symptoms of lung cancer

Lung cancer doesn't usually cause noticeable symptoms until it's spread through the lungs or into other parts of the body. This means the outlook for the condition isn't as good as many other types of cancer.

Overall, about 1 in 3 people with the condition live for at least a year after they're diagnosed and about 1 in 20 people live at least 10 years. However, survival rates can vary widely, depending on how far the cancer has spread at the time of diagnosis. Early diagnosis can make a big difference.

Symptoms of lung cancer develop as the condition progresses and there are usually no signs or symptoms in the early stages.

The main symptoms of lung cancer are listed below. If you have any of these, you should see your doctor:

- a cough that doesn't go away after two or three weeks
- a long-standing cough that gets worse
- persistent chest infections
- an ache or pain when breathing or coughing up blood
- persistent breathlessness and tiredness
- loss of appetite or unexplained weight loss

Less common symptoms of lung cancer include:

- changes in the appearance of your fingers, such as becoming more curved or their ends becoming larger (this is known as finger clubbing)

- a high temperature (fever) of 38C (100.4F) or above
- difficulty swallowing or pain when swallowing
- wheezing and hoarse voice
- swelling of your face or neck
- persistent chest or shoulder pain

## Causes of lung cancer

Most cases of lung cancer are caused by smoking, although people who have never smoked can also develop the condition.

### Smoking

Smoking cigarettes is the single biggest risk factor for lung cancer. It's responsible for more than 85% of all cases.

Tobacco smoke contains more than 60 different toxic substances, which can lead to the development of cancer. These substances are known to be carcinogenic (cancer-producing).

If you smoke more than 25 cigarettes a day, you are 25 times more likely to get lung cancer than a non-smoker.

While smoking cigarettes is the biggest risk factor, using other types of tobacco products can also increase your risk of developing lung cancer and other types of cancer, such as oesophageal cancer and mouth cancer. These products include:

- cigars
- pipe tobacco
- snuff (a powdered form of tobacco)
- chewing tobacco

Smoking cannabis has also been linked to an increased risk of lung cancer. Most cannabis smokers mix their cannabis with tobacco. While they tend to smoke less than tobacco smokers, they usually inhale more deeply and hold the smoke in their lungs for longer.

It is been estimated that smoking four joints (homemade cigarettes mixed with cannabis) may be as damaging to the lungs as smoking 20 cigarettes.

Even smoking cannabis without mixing it with tobacco is potentially dangerous. This is because cannabis also contains substances that can cause cancer.

## Passive smoking

If you don't smoke, frequent exposure to other people's tobacco smoke (passive smoking) can increase your risk of developing lung cancer.

For example, research has found that non-smoking women who share their house with a smoking partner are 25% more likely to develop lung cancer than non-smoking women who live with a non-smoking partner.

## Radon

Radon is a naturally occurring radioactive gas that comes from tiny amounts of uranium present in all rocks and soils. It can sometimes be found in buildings.

If radon is breathed in, it can damage your lungs, particularly if you're a smoker. Radon is estimated to be responsible for about 3% of all lung cancer deaths in England.

## Occupational exposure and pollution

Exposure to certain chemicals and substances used in several occupations and industries has been linked to a slightly higher risk of developing lung cancer. These chemicals and substances include:

- arsenic
- asbestos
- beryllium
- cadmium
- coal and coke fumes
- silica
- nickel

Research also suggests that being exposed to large amounts of diesel fumes for many years may increase your risk of developing lung cancer by up to 50%. One study has shown that your risk of developing lung cancer increases by about a third if you live in an area with high levels of nitrogen oxide gases (mostly produced by cars and other vehicles).

## Diagnosing lung cancer

See your doctor if you have symptoms of lung cancer, such as breathlessness or a persistent cough.

Your doctor will ask about your general health and what symptoms you've been experiencing. They may examine you and ask you to breathe into a device called a spirometer, which measures how much air you breathe in and out.

You may be asked to have a blood test to rule out some of the possible causes of your symptoms, such as a chest infection.

**Chest X-ray**

A chest X-ray is usually the first test used to diagnose lung cancer. Most lung tumours show up on X-rays as a white-grey mass.

However, chest X-rays can't give a definitive diagnosis because they often can't distinguish between cancer and other conditions, such as a lung abscess (a collection of pus that forms in the lungs).

If your chest X-ray suggests you may have lung cancer, you should be referred to a specialist (if you haven't already) in chest conditions such as lung cancer. A specialist can carry out more tests to investigate whether you have lung cancer and, if you do, what type it is and how much it's spread.

## CT scan

A computerised tomography (CT) scan is usually carried out after a chest X-ray. A CT scan uses X-rays and a computer to create detailed images of the inside of your body.

Before having a CT scan, you'll be given an injection of a contrast medium. This is a liquid containing a dye that makes the lungs show up more clearly on the scan. The scan is painless and takes 10-30 minutes to complete.

## PET-CT scan

A PET-CT scan (which stands for positron emission tomography -computerised tomography) may be carried out if the results of the CT scan show you have cancer at an early stage.

The PET-CT scan can show where there are active cancer cells. This can help with diagnosis and treatment.

Before having a PET-CT scan, you'll be injected with a slightly radioactive material. You'll be asked to lie down on a table, which slides into the PET scanner. The scan is painless and takes around 30-60 minutes.

**Bronchoscopy and biopsy**

If the CT scan shows there might be cancer in the central part of your chest, you'll have a bronchoscopy. A bronchoscopy is a procedure that allows a doctor or nurse to remove a small sample of cells from inside your lungs.

During a bronchoscopy, a thin tube called a bronchoscope is used to examine your lungs and take a sample of cells (biopsy). The bronchoscope is passed through your mouth or nose, down your throat and into the airways of your lungs.

The procedure may be uncomfortable, but you'll be given a mild sedative beforehand to help you relax and a local anaesthetic to make your throat numb. The procedure is very quick and only takes a few minutes.

**Other types of biopsy**

If you're not able to have one of the biopsies described above, or you've had one and the results weren't clear, you may be offered a different type of biopsy. This may be a type of surgical biopsy such as a thoracoscopy or a mediastinoscopy, or a biopsy carried out using a needle inserted through your skin.

**These types of biopsy are described below.**

**Percutaneous needle biopsy**

A percutaneous needle biopsy involves removing a sample from a suspected tumour to test it at a laboratory for cancerous cells. The doctor carrying out the biopsy will use a CT scanner to guide a needle to the site of a suspected tumour through the skin. A local anaesthetic is used to numb the surrounding skin, and the needle is passed through your skin and into your lungs. The needle will then be used to remove a sample of tissue for testing.

**Thoracoscopy**

A thoracoscopy is a procedure that allows the doctor to examine a particular area of your chest and take tissue and fluid samples.

You're likely to need a general anaesthetic before having a thoracoscopy. Two or three small cuts will be made in your chest to pass a tube (similar to a bronchoscope) into your chest. The doctor will use the tube to look inside your chest and take samples. The samples will then be sent away for tests.

After a thoracoscopy, you may need to stay in hospital overnight while any further fluid in your lungs is drained out.

## Mediastinoscopy

A mediastinoscopy allows the doctor to examine the area between your lungs at the centre of your chest (mediastinum).

For this test, you'll need to have a general anaesthetic and stay in hospital for a couple of days. The doctor will make a small cut at the bottom of your neck so they can pass a thin tube into your chest.

The tube has a camera at the end, which enables the doctor to see inside your chest. They'll also be able to take samples of your cells and lymph nodes at the same time. The lymph nodes are tested because they're usually the first place that lung cancer spreads to.

## Staging

Once the above tests have been completed, it should be possible to work out what stage your cancer is, what this means for your treatment and whether it's possible to completely cure the cancer.

## Non-small-cell lung cancer

Non-small-cell lung cancer (the most common type) usually spreads more slowly than small-cell lung cancer and responds differently to treatment.

## Bowel cancer

Bowel cancer is a general term for cancer that begins in the large bowel. Depending on where the cancer starts, bowel cancer is sometimes called colon or rectal cancer .

Bowel cancer is one of the most common types of cancer diagnosed in the UK. Most people diagnosed with it are over the age of 60.

## Symptoms of bowel cancer

The three main symptoms of bowel cancer are:

- persistent blood in the stools – that occurs for no obvious reason or is associated with a change in bowel habit

- a persistent change in your bowel habit –
  which usually means going more often, with
  looser stools
- persistent lower abdominal (tummy) pain ,
  bloating or discomfort – that's always caused
  by eating and may be associated with loss of
  appetite or significant unintentional weight
  loss

The symptoms of bowel cancer can be subtle and don't necessarily make you feel ill.

However, it's worth waiting for a short time to see if they get better as the symptoms of bowel cancer are persistent.

If you're unsure whether to see your doctor, try the bowel cancer symptom checker.

Bowel cancer symptoms are also very common, and most people with them don't have cancer.

For example:

- blood in the stools when associated with pain or soreness is more often caused by piles (haemorrhoids)
- a change in bowel habit or abdominal pain is usually the result of something you've eaten
- a change in bowel habit to going less often, with harder stools, is not usually caused by any serious condition – it may be worth trying laxatives before seeing your doctor

These symptoms should be taken more seriously as you get older and when they persist despite simple treatments.

**When to seek medical advice**

Try the bowel cancer symptom checker for advice on what you can try to see if your symptoms get better, and when you should see your doctor to discuss whether tests are necessary.

Your doctor may decide to:

- carry out a simple examination of your tummy and bottom to make sure you have no lumps
- arrange for a simple blood test to check for iron deficiency anaemia – this can indicate whether there's any bleeding from your bowel that you haven't been aware of
- arrange for you to have a simple test in hospital to make sure there's no serious cause of your symptoms

Make sure you see your doctor if your symptoms persist or keep coming back after stopping treatment, regardless of their severity or your age. You'll probably be referred to hospital.

## Causes of bowel cancer

It's not known exactly what causes bowel cancer, but there are a number of things that can increase your risk.

These include:

- age: almost 9 in 10 cases of bowel cancer occur in people aged 60 or over
- diet: a diet high in red or processed meats and low in fibre can increase your risk
- weight: bowel cancer is more common in people who are overweight or obese
- exercise: being inactive increases your risk of getting bowel cancer

- alcohol and smoking: a high alcohol intake and smoking may increase your chances of getting bowel cancer
- family history: having a close relative (mother or father, brother or sister) who developed bowel cancer under the age of 50 puts you at a greater lifetime risk of developing the condition; screening is offered to people in this situation, and you should discuss this with your doctor

Some people also have an increased risk of bowel cancer because they have another condition, such as extensive ulcerative colitis or Crohn's disease in the colon for more than 10 years.

Although there are some risks you can't change, such as your family history or your age, there are several ways you can lower your chances of developing the condition.

## Bowel cancer screening

Taking part in bowel cancer screening reduces your chances of dying from bowel cancer. Removing any polyps found in bowel scope screening can prevent cancer.

However, all screening involves a balance of potential harms, as well as benefits. It's up to you to decide if you want to have it.

To help you decide, read our pages on bowel cancer screening, which explain what the two tests involve, what the different possible results mean, and the potential risks for you to weigh up.

## Treatment for bowel cancer

Bowel cancer can be treated using a combination of different treatments, depending on where the cancer is in your bowel and how far it has spread.

The main treatments are:

- surgery – the cancerous section of bowel is removed; it's the most effective way of curing bowel cancer and in many cases is all you need
- chemotherapy – where medication is used to kill cancer cells
- radiotherapy – where radiation is used to kill cancer cells
- biological treatments – a newer type of medication that increases the effectiveness of chemotherapy and prevents the cancer spreading

As with most types of cancer, the chance of a complete cure depends on how far it has advanced by the time it's diagnosed. If the cancer is confined to the bowel, surgery is usually able to completely remove it.

Keyhole or robotic surgery is being used more often, which allows surgery to be performed with less pain and a quicker recovery.

## Bladder cancer

Bladder cancer is where a growth of abnormal tissue, known as a tumour, develops in the lining of the bladder. In some cases, the tumour spreads into the surrounding muscles.

The most common symptom of bladder cancer is blood in your urine, which is usually painless.

If you notice blood in your urine, even if it comes and goes, you should visit your doctor so the cause can be investigated.

Read more about the symptoms of bladder cancer.

## Types of bladder cancer

Once diagnosed, bladder cancer can be classified by how far it has spread.

If the cancerous cells are contained inside the lining of the bladder, doctors describe it as superficial or non-muscle invasive bladder cancer. This is the most common type of bladder cancer, accounting for 7 out of 10 cases. Most people do not die as a result this type of bladder cancer.

When the cancerous cells spread beyond the lining into the surrounding muscles of the bladder, it's referred to as muscle invasive bladder cancer. This is less common but has a higher chance of spreading to other parts of the body and can be fatal.

## Why does bladder cancer happen?

Most cases of bladder cancer appear to be caused by exposure of the bladder to harmful substances which, over the course of many years, lead to abnormal changes in the bladder's cells. Tobacco smoke is a common cause, it is estimated that half of all cases of bladder cancer are caused by smoking.

Contact with certain chemicals previously used in manufacturing is also known to cause bladder cancer. However, these substances have since been banned.

## Symptoms of bladder cancer

Blood in your urine is the most common symptom of bladder cancer.

The medical name for this is haematuria and it is usually painless. You may notice streaks of blood in your urine or the blood may turn your urine brown. The blood is not always noticeable and it may come and go.

Less common symptoms of bladder cancer include:

- a need to urinate on a more frequent basis
- sudden urges to urinate
- a burning sensation when passing urine

If bladder cancer reaches an advanced stage and begins to spread, symptoms can include:

- pelvic pain
- bone pain
- unexplained weight loss
- swelling of the legs

## When to seek medical advice

If you ever have blood in your urine - even if it comes and goes - you should visit your doctor so that the cause can be investigated.

Having blood in your urine does not mean that you definitely have bladder cancer, as there are other more common causes. These include a bladder infection (such as cystitis), kidney stones or an enlarged prostate gland (in men).

## Bladder cancer causes

Bladder cancer is caused by changes to the cells of the bladder. It is often linked with exposure to certain chemicals.

Cancer begins with a change (mutation) in the structure of the DNA in cells, which can affect how they grow. This means cells grow and reproduce uncontrollably, producing a lump of tissue called a tumour.

## Increased risk

It is not always known what causes the cell changes that lead to bladder cancer, but several things have been identified that can significantly increase your risk of developing it.

## Smoking

Smoking is the single biggest risk factor for bladder cancer. This because tobacco contains cancer-causing (carcinogenic) chemicals.

If you smoke for many years, these chemicals pass into your blood stream and are filtered by the kidneys into your urine. The bladder is repeatedly exposed to these harmful chemicals as it acts as a store for urine. This can cause changes to the cells of the bladder lining that may lead to bladder cancer.

It is estimated around half of all cases of bladder cancer are related to smoking, and people who smoke may be up to six times more likely to develop bladder cancer than non-smokers.

**Exposure to chemicals**

Exposure to certain industrial chemicals is the second biggest risk factor. Previous studies have estimated this may account for around 25% of cases.

Chemicals known to increase the risk of bladder cancer include:

- aniline dyes
- 2-Naphthylamine
- 4-Aminobiphenyl
- xenylamine
- benzidine

Occupations linked to an increased risk of bladder cancer are manufacturing jobs involving:

- dyes
- textiles
- rubbers
- paints
- plastics
- leather tanning

Some non-manufacturing jobs have also been linked to an increased risk of bladder cancer. These include taxi or bus drivers, due to their regular exposure to chemicals in diesel fumes.

The link between bladder cancer and these types of occupations was discovered in the 1950s and 1960s. Since then, regulations relating to exposure to cancer-causing chemicals have been made much more rigorous and many of the above chemicals have been banned.

However, these chemicals are still linked with cases of bladder cancer now, as it can take up to 30 years after initial exposure to the chemicals before the condition starts to develop.

**Other risk factors**
Other things known to increase your risk of bladder cancer include having:

- radiotherapy to treat previous cancers near the bladder, such as bowel cancer
- previous treatment with certain chemotherapy medications, such as cyclophosphamide and cisplatin
- a tube in your bladder (an in-dwelling catheter) for a long time because you have nerve damage that has resulted in paralysis
- a long-term or repeated urinary tract infection (UTI)
- an untreated infection called schistosomiasis, caused by a parasite that lives in fresh water - this is very rare in the UK

**How does bladder cancer spread?**

Bladder cancer usually begins in the cells of the bladder lining. In some cases, it may then spread into surrounding bladder muscle. If the cancer penetrates this muscle, it can spread to other parts of the body, usually through the lymphatic system. If bladder cancer spreads to other parts of the body, such as other organs, it is known as metastatic bladder cancer.

## Diagnosing bladder cancer

If you have symptoms of bladder cancer, such as blood in your urine, you should see your doctor.

Your doctor may ask about your symptoms, family history and whether you have been exposed to any possible causes of bladder cancer - such as smoking.

In some cases, your doctor may request a urine sample so it can be tested in a laboratory for traces of blood, bacteria or abnormal cells (see below).

Your doctor may also carry out a physical examination of your rectum and vagina because bladder cancer sometimes causes a noticeable lump that presses against them.

If your doctor suspects bladder cancer, they will refer you to a hospital for further tests.

Some hospitals have specialist clinics for people with blood in their urine (haematuria), whereas others have specialist urology departments for people with urinary tract problems.

**At the hospital**

If you are referred to a hospital specialist, there are several tests you may have to check for bladder cancer. These are outlined below.

## Urine tests

You may be asked to provide a urine sample, so it can be checked for any infection or abnormal cells. The test for abnormal cells is called urinary cytology.

Urinary cytology is not 100% accurate. It can sometimes detect abnormal cells even though there is no cancer present (a false-positive result) or it can fail to detect abnormal cells when cancer is present (a false-negative result). Therefore, urinary cytology is used to help diagnose bladder cancer rather than providing a definitive diagnosis.

## Cystoscopy

A cystoscopy uses a thin tube with a camera and light at the end, known as a flexible cystoscope, to examine the inside of your bladder. The procedure usually takes about 5 minutes.

During a cystoscopy, a local anaesthetic gel is applied to your urethra (the tube through which you urinate) so you don't feel any pain. The gel also helps the cystoscope to pass into the urethra more easily.

**Biopsy**

If abnormalities are found in your bladder during a cystoscopy, it is likely you will be asked to return so a sample of bladder tissue can be removed for further testing. This is known as a biopsy.

A biopsy is often carried out using a procedure known as transurethral resection of a bladder tumour (TURBT). The procedure is carried out under general anaesthetic.

See treating bladder cancer for more information about the TURBT procedure.

**Further testing**

If the results of your biopsy show cancerous cells in the lining of your bladder, you may need further tests. These will help determine whether the cancer has spread beyond the lining of your bladder and, if so, how far it has spread.

Further tests can include:

- computerised tomography (CT) scan - a series of X-rays are taken to create a detailed picture of the inside of the body. You may be given an injection or drink of dye beforehand to highlight abnormal areas.
- an intravenous (IV) urogram - after dye is injected into your bloodstream, X-rays are

used to study it as it passes through your urinary system.

## Staging and grading

Once these tests have been completed, it should be possible to tell you the grade of the cancer and what stage it is.

Grading is a measurement of how likely a cancer is to spread. The grade of a cancer is usually described using a number system, ranging from G1-G3. High grade cancers are more likely to spread then low grade cancers.

Staging is a measurement of how far the cancer has spread. Lower stages cancers are smaller and have a better chance of successful treatment. The most widely used staging system for bladder cancer is known as the TNM system, where:

- T stands for how far into the bladder the tumour has grown
- N stands for whether the cancer has spread into nearby lymph nodes
- M stands for whether the cancer has spread into another parts of the body (metastasis), such as the lungs
- T stages

The T staging system is as follows:

- TIS or CIS (carcinoma in situ), a very early, high grade, cancer confined to the innermost layer of the bladder lining
- Ta, the cancer is just in the innermost layer of the bladder lining

- T1, the cancerous cells have started to grow into the connective tissue beyond the bladder lining

Bladder cancer up to the T1 stage is usually called early bladder cancer or non-muscle invasive bladder cancer. If the tumour grows larger than this, it is usually called muscle-invasive bladder cancer and is categorised as:

- T2, the cancer has grown through the connective tissue into the bladder muscle
- T3, the cancer has grown through the layer of muscles into the surrounding layer of fat

If the tumour grows larger than the T3 stage, it is considered to be advanced bladder cancer and is categorised as:

- T4, the cancer has spread outside the bladder into surrounding organs,

## N stages

The N staging system is as follows:

- N0, there is no cancerous cells in any of your lymph nodes
- N1, there are cancerous cells in just one of your lymph nodes in your pelvis
- N2, there are cancerous cells in two or more lymph nodes in your pelvis
- N3, there are cancerous cells in one or more of your lymph nodes (known as common iliac nodes) found in your groin

## M stages

There are only two options in the M system:

- M0, where the cancer has not spread to another part of the body
- M1, where the cancer has spread to another part of the body, such as the bones, lungs or liver

The TNM system can be difficult to understand, so don't be afraid to ask your care team questions about your test results and what they mean for your treatment and outlook.

## Treating bladder cancer

The treatment options for bladder cancer largely depend on how advanced the cancer is.

Treatments usually differ between early stage, non-muscle invasive bladder cancer and more advanced muscle invasive bladder cancer.

## Multidisciplinary teams (MDTs)

All hospitals use multidisciplinary teams (MDTs) to treat bladder cancer. These are teams of specialists that work together to make decisions about the best way to proceed with your treatment.

Members of your MDT may include:

- a urologist (a surgeon specialising in treating conditions affecting the urinary tract)
- clinical oncologist (a specialist in chemotherapy and radiotherapy)
- pathologist (a specialist in diseased tissue)
- radiologist
- specialist cancer nurse, who will usually be your first point of contact with the rest of the team

Deciding what treatment is best for you can be difficult. Your MDT will make recommendations, but remember that the final decision is yours.

Before discussing your treatment options, you may find it useful to write a list of questions to ask your MDT.

**These treatments are discussed in more detail below.**

**Surgery**

The standard surgical treatment for non-muscle invasive bladder cancer is known as transurethral resection of a bladder tumour (TURBT) procedure. In most cases, this can be performed at the same time as a biopsy.

TURBT is carried out under general anaesthetic. The surgeon uses an instrument called a cystoscope to locate the visible tumours and cuts them away from the lining of the bladder. The wounds are then sealed (cauterised) using a mild electric current.

If you experience significant bleeding afterwards, a flexible tube called a catheter may be inserted into your urethra and passed up into your bladder. The catheter will be used to drain away any blood and debris from your bladder and may be kept in place for several days.

Most people are able to leave hospital less than 48 hours after having TURBT and are able to resume normal physical activity within two weeks.

## Chemotherapy

After surgery, you may be given a dose of chemotherapy directly into your bladder. This will be after you have recovered from the effects of the general anaesthetic.

A different type of chemotherapy (intravesical chemotherapy) is used directly into your bladder using a catheter (rather than affecting the whole body). The solution is kept in your bladder for about an hour before being drained away.

Some residue of the chemotherapy medication may be left in your urine which could severely irritate your skin. It helps to urinate while sitting down and be careful not to splash yourself or the toilet seat. After passing urine, wash the skin around your genitals with soap and water.

Side effects of intravesical chemotherapy can include a skin rash or irritation and inflammation of the bladder lining. This can cause a frequent need to urinate and pain when urinating. However, this should pass within a few days. You may also feel very tired or develop a rash.

If your cancer is at a low risk of spreading, you should not need additional chemotherapy treatment. However, if there is a moderate or high risk of the cancer spreading, you may be given additional courses of chemotherapy, usually once a week over six weeks.

If you are sexually active, it is important that you use a barrier method of contraception, such as a condom, while you are having intravesical chemotherapy. This is because the medication may be present in your semen or vaginal fluids, which can cause irritation.

You also shouldn't try to get pregnant or father a child while having intravesical chemotherapy, as the medication can increase the risk of having a child with birth defects.

### Bacillus Calmette-Guérin (BCG) treatment

After surgery, you may also be treated with a variant of the BCG vaccine. This is used to help prevent recurrence of bladder cancer when there is a high risk it returning.

The BCG vaccine was originally used to treat tuberculosis (TB), but it has also proved to be an effective treatment against bladder cancer. Exactly how the BCG vaccine works is still unclear.

The BCG vaccine is given in the same way as intravesical chemotherapy. The vaccine is passed into your bladder through a catheter and left in your bladder for two hours before being drained away.

As with intravesical chemotherapy, you should take precautions - such as sitting down while urinating to ensure that urine does not get onto your skin or the toilet seat.

Most people require weekly treatments over a six-week period. Depending on your circumstances, maintenance therapy may also be recommended. This involves receiving further doses of the BCG once a week for three weeks, with six month intervals.

Maintenance therapy usually lasts for three years.

Chemotherapy is usually preferred to BCG treatment because the side effects are less severe. Common side effects of BCG can include:

- a frequent need to urinate
- pain when urinating
- blood in your urine (haematuria)
- flu-like symptoms, such as tiredness, fever and aching
- urinary tract infections
- Muscle-invasive bladder cancer

**Cancer of the womb (uterus)**

Cancer of the womb (uterus) is a common cancer that affects the female reproductive system. It is also called uterine cancer and endometrial cancer.

Abnormal vaginal bleeding is the most common symptom of womb cancer.

If you have been through the menopause, any vaginal bleeding is considered to be abnormal. If you have not yet been through the menopause, unusual bleeding may include bleeding between your periods.

You should see you doctor as soon as possible if you experience any unusual vaginal bleeding. While it is unlikely that it is caused by womb cancer, it is best to be sure.

Your doctor will examine you and ask about your symptoms. If they suspect you may have a serious problem or if they are unsure about a diagnosis, they will refer you to a specialist for further tests.

Read more about the symptoms of womb cancer and diagnosing womb cancer.

**Types of womb cancer**

The vast majority of womb cancers begin in the cells that make up the lining of the womb (called the endometrium), which is why cancer of the womb is often called endometrial cancer.

In rare cases, womb cancer can start in the muscles surrounding the womb. This type of cancer is called uterine sarcoma and may be treated in a different way to endometrial cancer.

Womb cancer is separate from other cancers of the female reproductive system, such as ovarian cancer and cervical cancer.

## Why does womb cancer happen?

It is not clear exactly what causes womb cancer, but certain things can increase your risk of developing the condition.

A hormone imbalance is one of the most important risks for womb cancer. Specifically, your risk is increased if you have high levels of a hormone called oestrogen in your body.

A number of things can cause this hormone imbalance, including the menopause, obesity, diabetes and hormone replacement therapy (HRT). There is also a small increase in the risk of womb cancer with long-term use of the breast cancer drug tamoxifen.

It is not always possible to prevent womb cancer, but some things are thought to reduce your risk.

This includes maintaining a healthy weight and the long-term use of some types of contraception.

## How is womb cancer treated?

The most common treatment for womb cancer is the surgical removal of the womb (hysterectomy). A hysterectomy can cure womb cancer in its early stages, but you will no longer be able to get pregnant. Surgery for womb cancer is also likely to include the removal of the ovaries and fallopian tubes.

Radiotherapy or chemotherapy are also sometimes used, often in conjunction with surgery.

A type of hormone therapy may be used if you are yet to go through the menopause and would still like to have children.

Even if your cancer is advanced and the chances of a cure are small, treatment can still help to relieve symptoms and prolong your life.

## Womb cancer symptoms

In 90% of cases, womb cancer causes abnormal bleeding from the vagina.

Bleeding may start as light bleeding accompanied by a watery discharge, which may get heavier over time. Most women diagnosed with womb cancer have been through the menopause, so any vaginal bleeding will be unusual.

In women who haven't been through the menopause, unusual vaginal bleeding may consist of:

- periods that are heavier than usual
- vaginal bleeding inbetween normal periods

Less common symptoms include pain in the lower abdomen (tummy) and pain during sex.

If womb cancer reaches a more advanced stage, it may cause additional symptoms. These include:

- pain in the back, legs or pelvis
- loss of appetite
- tiredness
- nausea

## When to seek medical advice

If you have postmenopausal vaginal bleeding or notice a change in the normal pattern of your period, visit your doctor.

Only 1 in 10 cases of unusual vaginal bleeding after the menopause are caused by womb cancer, so it's unlikely your symptoms will be caused by this condition.

However, if you have unusual vaginal bleeding, it is important to get the cause of your symptoms investigated. The bleeding may be the result of a number of other potentially serious health conditions, such as polyps or fibroids (non-cancerous growths that can develop inside the uterus). Other types of gynaecological cancer can also cause unusual vaginal bleeding, particularly cervical cancer.

## Can a Ketogenic Diet Help Fight Cancer?

Cancer is the second leading cause of death in the United States.

Researchers estimated that 606,520 Americans would die from cancer in 2020. That means more than 1,600 deaths a day, on average.

Cancer is most commonly treated with a combination of surgery, chemotherapy, and radiation.

Many different diet strategies have been studied, but none has been particularly effective.

Interestingly, some early research suggests that a very low carb ketogenic diet may help.

Important note: You should never, ever delay or avoid conventional medical treatment of cancer in favor of an alternative treatment such as the ketogenic diet. You should discuss all treatment options with your healthcare provider.

## A brief overview of the ketogenic diet

The ketogenic diet is a very low carb, high fat diet that shares many similarities with other low carb diets, like the Atkins diet.

It involves significantly reducing your intake of carbs and replacing them with fat and protein. This change leads to a metabolic state called ketosis.

After several days, fat becomes your body's primary energy source.

This causes a substantial increase in the levels of compounds called ketones in your blood (5).

In general, a ketogenic diet provides 70% of calories as fat, with 20% of calories from protein and 10% of calories from carbs.

There are many versions of the ketogenic diet, though. Some versions are even higher in fat.

The ketogenic diet is a very low carb, high fat diet. Fat intake may be 70% of total calorie intake, if not higher.

**The role of blood sugar in cancer**

Many cancer therapies are designed to target the biological differences between cancer cells and normal cells.

Nearly all cancer cells share one common trait: They feed off carbs or blood sugar in order to grow and multiply.

When you follow a ketogenic diet, some of the standard metabolic processes are altered, and your blood sugar levels go way down.

Basically, this is claimed to "starve" the cancer cells of fuel.

As in all living cells, the long-term effect of this "starvation" may be that the cancer cells will grow more slowly, decrease in size, or possibly even die.

It seems possible that a ketogenic diet could help reduce the progression of cancer because it causes a rapid decrease in blood sugar levels.

A ketogenic diet can lower blood sugar levels. This may help reduce tumor growth and even starve cancer cells of energy.

**Other benefits of a ketogenic diet to treat cancer**

Several other processes may explain how a ketogenic diet can aid cancer treatment.

Firstly, reducing carbs can quickly lower calorie intake, reducing the energy available to the cells in your body.

In turn, this may slow tumor growth and the cancer's progression.

In addition, ketogenic diets can provide other benefits.

## Lowered insulin

Insulin is an anabolic hormone. This means that insulin makes cells, including cancerous cells, grow when it's present. Therefore, lower insulin levels may slow tumor growth.

## Increased ketones

Cancer cells can't use ketones as fuel. Research in animals shows that ketones may reduce tumor size and growth.

Beyond lowering blood sugar, the ketogenic diet may also help treat cancer via other mechanisms. These include lowering calories, reducing insulin levels, and increasing ketones.

## The ketogenic diet and cancer in humans

Despite the promising evidence in animals, research in humans is only just emerging and largely limited to case studies.

Currently, the limited research seems to show that a ketogenic diet may reduce tumor size and the progression rate of certain cancers.

### Brain cancer studies

Much of the research on cancer looks at glioblastomas, which are particularly aggressive brain tumors.

A 2010 case study marked the first time that research was published on the effects of treating a glioblastoma with a combination of standard therapy and a restricted ketogenic diet.

The case study followed a 65-year-old woman. Following surgery, she received a very low calorie ketogenic diet. During this time, the tumor's progression slowed.

However, 10 weeks after returning to a normal diet, she experienced a significant increase in tumor growth.

Results from later research are also promising. Almost all of the later research has concluded that a ketogenic diet leads to reduced glucose levels.

In addition, the studies showed that a ketogenic diet is safe and may help to enhance the effects of traditional cancer treatments.

In another study, 3 out of 5 people with a glioma experienced complete remission after adopting a ketogenic diet combined with radiation or chemotherapy.

The other two participants, though, experienced a progression in the disease after they stopped the ketogenic diet.

Similar case reports from 1995 examined the reactions to a ketogenic diet in two girls who were undergoing treatment for advanced brain cancer.

Researchers found that glucose uptake was decreased in the tumors of both girls.

One of the girls reported improved quality of life and remained on the diet for 12 months. During that time, her disease showed no further progression.

## Studies of other cancers

Following a ketogenic diet for 12 weeks significantly increased the physical function of women with ovarian or endometrial cancer.

Some participants in the study followed the high fiber, low fat American Cancer Society (ACS) diet instead. The women who followed the ketogenic diet were more likely to report that they could readily complete activities such as climbing stairs or moving a table.

They also experienced other benefits, such as increased energy and decreased cravings for starchy foods and "fast food fats" like pizza.

The ketogenic diet may also help improve the body composition of people with various types of cancer.

In a study of 81 people, researchers observed benefits such as reduced fat mass in people with rectal or breast cancer and the preservation of skeletal muscle mass.

Study participants experienced these benefits even though they were also undergoing radiation therapy, chemotherapy, or a combination of both. These standard cancer treatments have been known to negatively affect body composition and appetite.

## Quality-of-life study

One quality-of-life study investigated the effects of a ketogenic diet in 16 people with advanced cancer.

Several people dropped out of the study because they did not enjoy the diet or due to personal reasons. Two people died early.

Out of the 16 participants, 5 remained on the ketogenic diet for the entire 3-month study period. They reported improved emotional well-being and reduced insomnia, without any negative side effects caused by the diet.

Some parameters, such as fatigue and pain, remained the same or worsened over time. Because the study participants all had advanced disease, this outcome was expected.

Although the ketogenic diet showed benefits for quality of life, the relatively low compliance rate indicates that it may be hard to get people to stick with the diet.

A few small studies and case reports in humans suggest that a ketogenic diet may help slow the progression of cancer. However, a lot more research is needed.

# The ketogenic diet and cancer prevention

Some mechanisms suggest that a ketogenic diet may help prevent the development of cancer in the first place.

Primarily, it may reduce several of the main risk factors for cancer.

## May decrease IGF-1 levels

Insulin-like growth factor 1 (IGF-1) is a hormone that's important for cell development. It also reduces programmed cell death.

This hormone plays a role in the development and progression of cancer.

The ketogenic diet reduces IGF-1 levels, thereby decreasing the direct effects insulin has on cell growth.

This may reduce tumor growth and cancer risk over the long term.

## Can help blood sugar levels and management of diabetes

Other evidence suggests that people with elevated blood sugar levels and diabetes have an increased risk of developing cancer.

Research shows that a ketogenic diet can be very effective at lowering blood sugar levels and managing diabetes, at least in the short term.

Some people may find it challenging to adhere to the diet over a long period of time, though. More studies on the long-term safety of the diet are also needed.

**May decrease obesity**

Obesity is also a risk factor for cancer.

Since a ketogenic diet is a powerful weight loss tool, it may also help reduce the risk of cancer by fighting obesity.

The ketogenic diet reduces IGF-1 levels, blood sugar levels, and the risk of diabetes and obesity. These factors may lead to a reduced risk of developing cancer in the first place.

## Possible disadvantages for people with cancer

It's important to note that no major cancer group recommends the ketogenic diet for either cancer prevention or cancer treatment, despite the promising research.

The ketogenic diet has its benefits, but it comes with risks, too.

For instance, the diet is very high in fat. In addition, many foods allowed on the diet, such as red meat, have been shown to increase the risk of some cancers. The diet is very limiting in terms of foods known to prevent cancer, such as whole grains, fruits, and some vegetables.

It can also be challenging for those undergoing traditional cancer therapies to consume enough calories while on the diet. Low carb diets, such as ketogenic diets, often result in weight loss.

Compliance is poor, which makes the diet challenging for people with cancer. The restrictive nature of the diet can sometimes be too much for a person with cancer, especially when food can be a source of comfort.

The diet isn't appropriate for everyone and could even cause harm. If you'd like to explore the ketogenic diet, speak with a medical professional first. They can help you decide whether the diet's right for you in the first place and work with you along the way.

A ketogenic diet provides many benefits for health. According to animal studies and some preliminary research in humans, it may also help treat or prevent cancer. However, it's important to keep in mind that the current research is still emerging.

You should never, ever avoid conventional cancer treatment in favor of an alternative treatment like the ketogenic diet.

Your best bet is still to follow the advice of your oncologist. Mainstream medical treatments are very effective at treating many common types of cancer.

That said, perhaps a ketogenic diet could be a good choice as an adjuvant therapy, meaning that it's used in addition to the conventional treatments.

**Side Effects, Risks, and Contraindications**

With any approach to cancer, the potential benefits must be weighed against risks. The same is true when thinking about adopting a keto diet. Here are some of the more common problems that arise.

## Side Effects

When people begin the keto diet, it's common to have symptoms that have been called the "keto flu." This can include fatigue, nausea, vomiting, a lower exercise tolerance, constipation, and other digestive system side effects.

## Risks

These side effects as well as the metabolic effects of the keto diet can pose some risks, including:

- Dehydration
- Kidney stones
- Gout
- Hypoglycemia

People should also be aware that keto can cause a false positive alcohol breath test.

Long term side effects may include low protein levels in the blood (hypoproteinemia), fatty liver disease, and low levels of key vitamins and minerals. Since the diet is hard to maintain, and research is relatively new, all of the potential longterm effects are unknown.

## Potential Risks Related to Cancer

While few studies have been done, the keto diet presents some possible risks for people with cancer. Here are a few to know, and discuss with a doctor, before making any diet changes.

## Dietary Needs and Possible Deficiencies

The keto diet is strict, and it could be hard to get all of the important nutrients needed in a healthy diet. The increase in fat intake could be a problem too. For example, a low-fat diet has been linked to a lower risk of recurrence with some types of breast cancer. On the other hand, keto may help some people lose weight; obesity is linked with a higher risk of breast cancer recurrence.

When you are coping with cancer, or if you have a hereditary disorder of fat metabolism, your body may not function the same way it does in people who are cancer-free. Just as cancer cells may be unable to process the proteins and fats, it's possible that healthy cells may have problems as well.

A significant concern is that of restricting foods such as fruits. There are many studies that have found a lower risk of cancer in people who eat a greater number of fruits and vegetables.

Since dairy products are restricted on some keto diets, a lack of vitamin D also may be a concern. That said, due to the association of low vitamin D levels with poorer outcomes in some cancers, everyone with cancer should have a blood test to determine their vitamin D level, and talk to their oncologist if the level is low (or within the low end of the normal range)

Dairy products are off-limits in some keto diets, and that means a lack of vitamin D may be a concern. Low vitamin D levels are associated with poorer outcomes in some cancers. Everyone with cancer should have a blood test of their vitamin D level, and talk to their oncologist if the level is low.

## Fiber

Since the ketogenic diet restricts fruits and legumes, it may also reduce fiber intake. Fiber can be thought of as a "prebiotic" or a food that feeds your gut bacteria.

For people with cancer treated with immunotherapy, a diverse gut microbiome is associated with greater effectiveness. Though probiotics did not appear to help, a high fiber diet did. Fiber also helps maintain bowel function. Current USDA guidelines recommend an intake of 23 to 33 grams of fiber daily.

## Fatigue

Keto could make fatigue associated with cancer (cancer fatigue) worse at the start, and many people considered this fatigue to be one of the more annoying side effects of cancer treatment.

## Cancer Cachexia

While praised as a method to lose weight, weight loss may be detrimental to someone living with cancer. Cancer cachexia, a syndrome of unintentional weight loss and muscle wasting, is thought to be the direct cause of 20% of cancer deaths.

## Contraindications

The keto diet should be avoided by women who are pregnant, wish to become pregnant, or are breastfeeding. It should also be used with caution in people with diabetes, and only under the careful guidance of a doctor. There are several medical conditions for which keto should absolutely not be used. These conditions include:

- Liver failure
- Pancreatitis
- Certain hereditary syndromes, such as pyruvate kinase deficiency, and other disorders of fat metabolism.

## Diet and Cancer

We know that what we eat is important. Just as higher octane gasoline may lead to better function in cars, our bodies function most efficiently when we give them the right fuel. When it comes down to diet and cancer, however, the research is in its infancy.

A diet high in fruits and vegetables and low in processed meats is linked to a lower risk of many cancers. Less is known about how specific foods and diets affect a cancer already present.

Fortunately, there are currently many clinical trials in place designed to answer these questions.

# Recipes for cancer diet

## Quinoa Porridge

Want to ensure a balanced blood sugar throughout the day and overnight?

Eat quinoa porridge for breakfast.

Quinoa porridge washes out the sugar in the bloodstream and transfers it into the cells to be converted to energy, therefore preventing the development of cancer cells.

### Ingredients
Maple syrup
Honey
Coconut palm sugar

1 cup of quinoa

1 cup of coconut milk

1.5 teaspoon of ginger

½ cup of cranberries/strawberries/blueberries/ raspberrie (dried, preferred)

½ cup of walnut, chopped

½ cup of hemp hearts

2 cups of water

2 pieces of apple, diced

3 teaspoons of cinnamon

**Instructions:**

Using a crock pot pour water and coconut milk. Combine quinoa, ginger, apples, and the preferred berries.

Stir over a low heat and let it simmer overnight.

When it is time for breakfast, pour on a bowl then top it with hemp hearts and walnuts.

Drizzle with the preferred syrup.

# Veggie Turmeric Muffins

Munch on some veggie turmeric muffins for breakfast.

This anti-cancer muffins contain turmeric which has anti-oxidant and anti inflammatory benefits that preprograms cell death.

Not only that, turmeric has pre-anti-cancer activities since it boosts the blood levels of vitamins C and E.

**Ingredients:**

Pepper

½ cup of coconut milk

1 teaspoon of turmeric

1 cup of spinach, chopped

1 teaspoon of sea salt

1 tablespoon of basil

1 cup of spinach

2 cups of tomatoes,

12 eggs

**Instructions:**

Preheat oven to 350 °F

Grease 12 muffin tins

Pour coconut milk and eggs on a bowl then whip.

Add in vegetables, spinach, basil, turmeric, sea salt, and pepper 5. Pour mixture onto muffin tins

Bake until edges are golden brown and the middle of the turmeric muffin is cooked

Can be stored in the refrigerator for a week.

## Anti-cancer Steamed Kale

Break faster by boiling Kale in as quick as 1, 2, 3 minutes.

Kale is an anti-cancer vegetable which is high in calcium, fiber, and low in carbohydrates.

**Ingredients:**

¼ cup of water

4 pieces of Kale leaves, washed and sliced

**Instructions:**

Using a pot, pour water and boil

Add Kale leaves and steam over high heat for 3 minutes

Drain water to prevent overcooking

## Apple Oatmeal

Prevent yourself from going to the doctor by eating an apple. That famous quote is true since the apple fruit is rich in anti-oxidants which washes away free radicals, thus reduces the risk of cancer.

## Ingredients:

Pinch of sea salt

1 piece of apple

1 cup of rolled oats

2 cups of apple juice

## Instructions:

Using a pan, pour apple juice and sprinkle sea salt.
Add in rolled oats and apple then bring to a boil.
Turn heat low and simmer uncovered for 10
minutes

# Blueberry Muesli Oatmeal and Apple Juice

## Ingredients:

Water

1 ½ cup of rolled oats

½ cup of walnuts, chopped

½ cup of apples, dried and chopped

2 cups of blueberries

2 teaspoons of cinnamon powder

3 tablespoons of brown sugar

**Instructions:**

Preheat oven to 325 °F

Using a bowl, pour water and mix in oats, sugar, and cinnamon powder.

Pour mixture evenly onto a non stick baking tray 4.

Toast mixture in the pre heated oven for 10 minutes, stirring occasionally.

Remove from oven and pour onto a large bowl 6.

Mix in dried apples and chopped walnuts 7. Divide mixture equally onto bowls

## Indian Spiced Roasted Cauliflower

Cauliflower and Indian spiced herbs is a great anti-cancer combination.

## Ingredients:

¼ cup of coconut milk

½ teaspoon of black pepper

1 head of cauliflower

1 tablespoon of cumin

1 tablespoon of garlic powder

2 tablespoons of turmeric

2 tablespoon chili powder

2 teaspoon of sea salt

1 tablespoon of lime juice

1 tablespoon of lemon zest

## Instructions:

Preheat oven for 400 °F then grease coconut oil on a baking sheet 2. Trim the cauliflower's base, stem and green leaves 3. Using a bowl, pour coconut milk and lemon zest. Then mix in lemon zest, turmeric, cumin, chili powder, garlic powder, sea salt, and black pepper

Dip the cauliflower onto the mixture to coat the head 5. Place cauliflower on the baking sheet and roast for 40 minutes, until the exterior is fried
Let it sit and slice into wedges

## Lamb Burger with Kalamata and Gremolata

Who says anti-cancer dieters are not allowed to eat meat? Good news, lamb meat is a supermeat because ounces of it brings the following benefits:

- Selenium cancer fighter
- Vitamin B12 good for the heart
- Monounsaturated fats good fat
- Conjugated linolenic acid fat burner
- Omega – 3 fats

**Ingredients:**
½ teaspoon of Celtic sea salt

½ teaspoon of oregano, dried

½ teaspoon of black pepper

1/3 cup of kalamata olives

¼ cup of parsley

1 ½ pound of ground lamb, grass - fed

1 piece of lemon

1 tablespoon of extra virgin olive oil

1 lemon zest

2 tablespoon of lemon juice

8 tablespoons of mint

**Instructions:**

Prepare gremolata mixture by combining parsley, mint, garlic, lemon juice and zest. Set aside

Using a bowl, combine ground lamb, kalamata olives, oregano, celtic sea salt, and black pepper

Form ½ inch thick lamb burger patties then cook on the grill pan for 5 minutes

Serve with the gremolata mixture

# Spaghetti Pomodoro

Spaghetti for the anti-cancer dieters, the spaghetti pomodoro is made up of zucchini the freshest, organic, and dairy free ingredients to satisfy your spaghetti cravings.

## Ingredients:

¼ teaspoon of Celtic sea salt

1 zucchini, organic

2 tomatoes

2 tablespoon of extra virgin olive oil

3 cloves of garlic

10 leaves of basil

## Instructions:

Make the spaghetti by cutting the zucchini in widthwise and process through a Saladacco

Slice tomatoes and place it in a food processor together with the garlic and basil. Process for 30 seconds using the S blade 3. Pour mixture onto a bowl then mix in olive and salt 4. Pour the sauce over the zucchini

## Anti-cancer Dill Cheese

A dill cheese may be a simple anti-cancer lunch recipe, but it's a one strong fighter because of its fresh and organic ingredients.

### Ingredients:

½ cup of water

¼ teaspoon of Celtic sea salt

2 cups of sunflower seeds, raw

2 tablespoon of lemon juice

2 cloves of garlic

2 tablespoons of dill

**Instructions:**

Using a blender, pour lemon juice then add dill, garlic, and sea salt.

Blend on low speed while pouring water until desired consistency 3. Serve as a dressing on preferred fresh green salad 4. Store in an air – tight container for up to 3 days

## Mediterranean Spaghetti

This is a delicious dish that is packed full of an authentic Mediterranean flavor I know you will fall in love with.

**Ingredient List:**

1 red bell pepper, chopped

1 yellow bell pepper, chopped

2 plum tomatoes, chopped

12 cherry tomatoes, chopped

1 zucchini, chopped

1 handful of baby spinach

1 handful of black olives, pits removed and chopped

2 Tablespoons of pureed tomato

½ of a jalapeno pepper, chopped

2 Tablespoons of dried herbs de provence

2 Tablespoons of apple cider vinegar

Dash of salt

1 box of gluten free spaghetti

**Instructions:**

In a saucepan set over medium to high heat, add in 2 tablespoons of olive oil, chopped red bell pepper, chopped yellow bell pepper, chopped plum tomatoes, chopped cherry tomatoes and chopped zucchini. Allow to come to a simmer. Cook for 10 minutes or until the vegetables are soft.

Add in the pureed tomato and apple cider vinegar. Stir well to incorporate.

Prepare the pasta according to the directions on the package. Once cooked, drain the pasta and set aside.

Add in the baby spinach and cooked pasta. Toss well to mix. Cook for 5 minutes.

Add in the chopped jalapeno pepper, dried herbs de provence and dash of salt. Toss again. Cook for an additional 2 minutes.

Remove from heat and serve immediately.

## Broiled Citrus Salad

This is a sweet tasting salad that is great for a lunch time meal. One bite and I know you will become hooked.

### Ingredient List:

3 oranges, cut into segments

1 grapefruit, cut into segments

¼ cup of feta cheese, crumbled

3 Tablespoons of mint leaves, chopped

2 Tablespoons of extra virgin olive oil

½ teaspoons of sea salt

**Instructions:**

On a baking sheet, add the orange and grapefruit segments.

Place into the oven to broil for 5 minutes or until lightly charred. Remove and transfer onto a plate.

Top off with the chopped leaves and a drizzle of the olive oil.

Season with a dash of sea salt.

Serve immediately.

## Farmer's Market Salad

This is a healthy salad dish you can make whenever you are craving something on the healthier side.

## Ingredient List:

2 cups of zucchini, thinly sliced

1 cup of yellow wax beans, chopped into pieces

1 cup of sugar snap peas, trimmed

1 cup of radishes, thinly sliced

½ of a kohlrabi, cut into halves and thinly sliced

1 cup of flat leaf parsley, chopped

1 spring onion, thinly sliced

Dash of chives, chopped

2 Tablespoons of sunflower seeds, toasted

## Ingredients for the dressing:

2 Tablespoons of flax oil

2 teaspoons of apple cider vinegar

1 teaspoon of tamari, extra for taste

Dash of sea salt

## Instructions:

In a steamer basket set over a pot filled with boiling water, add in the sliced zucchini, yellow wax beans, sliced radishes and sliced kohlrabi. Steam for 2 minutes or until slightly crispy. Spread onto a plate. Steam the sugar snap peas for 1 minute. Transfer onto a plate.

On the plate, add in the chopped flat leaf parsley, sliced spring onion, chopped chives and toasted sunflower seeds. Toss well to mix.

Prepare the dressing. In a bowl, add in the flax oil, apple cider vinegar, dash of sea salt and tamari. Whisk well until mixed.

Pour the dressing over the salad. Serve immediately.

## Quinoa Carrot Cakes

Make these delicious cakes whenever you need a sweet treat to snack on. It is great for those who have a strong sweet tooth that need to be satisfied.

**Ingredient List:**

8 apricots, chopped

1 banana, mashed

2 handfuls of walnuts, whole

½ cup of apple juice

4 Tablespoons of brown rice syrup

3 Tablespoons of milled flaxseed

2 Tablespoons of extra virgin olive oil

1 cup of carrots, grated

Dash of sea salt

½ cup of quinoa flour

¾ cup of brown rice flour

2 teaspoons of baker's style baking powder

2 teaspoons of powdered cinnamon

1 tablespoon of coconut sugar

¼ teaspoons of powdered cinnamon, for topping

**Instructions:**

Preheat the oven to 350 degrees. Line a muffin pan with paper muffin liners.

In a bowl, add in the apple juice, chopped apricots, mashed banana, whole walnuts, brown rice syrup, milled flaxseed and extra virgin olive oil. Stir well to mix.

Add in the grated carrots and sea salt. Stir well to incorporate and set aside.

In a separate bowl, add in the quinoa flour, baker's style baking powder and powdered cinnamon. Stir to mix. Add the banana mix into it and stir well until evenly mixed.

Spoon the mix into the muffin pan, filling each cup ¾ of the way full.

Place into the oven to bake for 40 minutes or until baked through. Remove and set onto a wire rack to cool completely.

In a separate bowl, add in the coconut sugar and powdered cinnamon. Stir well to mix. Sprinkle this mix over each of the cakes.

Serve.

## Spaghetti Squash with Parsley Pesto and Shrimp

This is a light and hearty squash dish that you don't have to feel guilty about. It is made with shrimp, making it perfect for those shrimp lovers out there.

**Ingredient List:**

1, 4 pound of spaghetti squash

1 to 2 Tablespoons of extra virgin olive oil

Dash of salt and black pepper

**Ingredients for the pesto sauce:**

½ cup of basil leaves, chopped

½ cup of parsley leaves, chopped

2 cloves of garlic, minced

1/3 cup of pine nuts

¼ teaspoons of salt

½ cup of extra virgin olive oil

**Ingredients for the shrimp:**

1 pound of shrimp, peeled and deveined

2 Tablespoons of extra virgin olive oil

3 cloves of garlic, minced

**Ingredients for the serving:**

Pine nuts, chopped

Lemon wedges

Grated parmesan cheese

**Instructions:**

Prepare the squash. Preheat the oven to 400 degrees.

Chop the ends off of the spaghetti squash and slice in half lengthwise. Scoop out the seeds and brush the insides of the squash with olive oil. Season with a dash of salt and black pepper.

Place the squash with the cut side facing down onto a baking sheet. Place into the oven to bake for 45 to 50 minutes or until soft. Remove and set aside to cool completely. Scrape the flesh until spaghetti tendrils form. Transfer the tendrils into a bowl and set aside.

Prepare the sauce. In a food processor, add in all of the ingredients for the sauce. Blend on the highest setting until smooth in consistency.

Prepare the shrimp. In a skillet set over medium heat, add in 1 tablespoon of olive oil. Add in the shrimp and garlic. Cook for 1 to 2 minutes or until the shrimp begins to turn pink. Flip and continue to cook for an additional 1 to 2 minutes or until the shrimp is cooked through.

Lower the heat to low. Add in the spaghetti squash and pesto sauce. Stir well to mix. Cook for 3 minutes or until hot. Remove from heat.

Serve with a topping of pine nuts, lemon wedges and grated parmesan cheese over the top.

## Sweet Potato and Apple Soup

This is another great tasting soup recipe you can make whenever you are feeling sick to your stomach. It is light enough and will help to settle your stomach.

**Ingredient List:**

2 Tablespoons of extra virgin olive oil

2 sweet potatoes, chopped

2 to 3 carrots, chopped

1 apple, core removed and chopped

1 onion, chopped

1 clove of garlic, crushed

½ cup of red lentils

¼ teaspoons of dried ginger

½ teaspoons of powdered cumin

½ teaspoons of powdered chili

½ teaspoons of smoked paprika

Dash of salt

4 cups of vegetable broth

2 sprigs of thyme, chopped

Plain yogurt, for garnish

**Instructions:**

In a pot set over medium to high heat, add in the olive oil. Add in the chopped sweet potatoes, chopped carrots, chopped apple, crushed garlic and chopped onion. Stir well to mix. Cook for 5 minutes or until translucent.

Add in the red lentils, dried ginger, powdered cumin, powdered chili, smoked paprika and dash of salt. Stir well to mix.

Add in the vegetable broth.

Allow to come to a boil. Lower the heat to low. Cook for 30 minutes or until the vegetables are soft.

Transfer the soup into a blender. Blend on the highest setting until smooth in consistency. Pour back into the pot. Allow to come back to a simmer. Serve the soup with a garnish of chopped thyme and dollop of plain yogurt.

## Sautéed Chicken with Wild Mushrooms and Kale

This is an easy and savory chicken dish that is impossible to resist. It is made with healthy kale and wild mushrooms, giving it even more flavor.

**Ingredient List:**

1 pound of kale, cut into pieces

1 tablespoon of all-purpose flour

2 teaspoons of butter, soft

1 tablespoon + 2 teaspoons of extra virgin olive oil

4, 6 ounce chicken breasts, boneless, skinless and pounded

Dash of salt and black pepper

½ pound of wild mushrooms, thinly sliced

3 shallots, minced

1/3 cup of dried white wine

2/3 cup of chicken stock

2 teaspoons of lemon juice

**Instructions:**

In a pot set over medium to high heat, fill with water. Allow to come to a boil. Add in the kale and blanch for 2 minutes. Drain and set aside.

In a bowl, add in the all-purpose flour and butter. Stir well until smooth in consistency.

In a skillet set over medium to high heat, add in the olive oil. Season the chicken breasts with a dash of salt and black pepper. Add into the skillet. Cook for 4 minutes on each side or until browned. Transfer onto a plate and set aside.

In the skillet, add in 1 teaspoon of olive oil. Add in the sliced wild mushrooms, minced shallots, 2 tablespoons of water, dash of salt and black pepper. Stir well to mix. Cook for 8 minutes or until the mushrooms are soft.

Pour the dried white wine into the skillet. Deglaze the bottom of the pan.

Add in the chicken stock. Cook for 3 minutes. Add in the flour mix and stir well until thick in consistency.

Add in the mushroom mix and cook for 2 minutes or until hot. Transfer this mix into a bowl.

Clean the skillet. Set over high heat. Add in 1 teaspoon of olive oil. Add in the kale. Season with a dash of salt and black pepper. Cook for 3 minutes or until browned. Add in the lemon juice and stir well to mix. Remove from heat.

Serve the chicken with a topping of the mushrooms and the kale mix.

## Walnut Crusted Tilapia

This is a great tasting fish you can make to enjoy the crispiness of natural fish with a healthy and nutty twist with the use of crushed walnuts.

### Ingredient List:

1 tablespoon of extra virgin olive oil, evenly divided

1 egg

1 lemon, zest only

1 clove of garlic, chopped

1 tablespoon of grated Parmesan cheese

Dash of salt and black pepper

¼ cup of walnuts, chopped

2/3 cup of whole wheat breadcrumbs

1 pound of tilapia fillets

**Instructions:**

Preheat the oven to 425 degrees. Grease a baking dish with 1 teaspoon of olive oil.

In a bowl, add in the egg. Whisk until lightly beaten.

Add in the lemon zest, the remaining extra virgin olive oil, chopped garlic, grated parmesan cheese, dash of salt and black pepper. Stir well to mix.

Add in the chopped walnuts and breadcrumbs in a separate bowl. Stir well to mix.

Dip the tilapia fillets in the egg mix. Roll in the breadcrumb and walnut mixture until coated on all sides. Place into the baking dish.

Place into the oven to bake for 15 to 20 minutes or until baked through.

Remove and rest for 5 minutes before serving.

## Oven Roasted Chickpeas

This is a simple and delicious chickpea dish that you can make whenever you are craving something with a ton of flavor.

**Ingredient List:**

1, 14 ounce can of chickpeas, drained

1 red onion, chopped

2 bananas, thinly sliced

1 tablespoon of powdered curry

1 teaspoon of coriander seeds

2 to 3 Tablespoons of extra virgin coconut oil

1 bunch of cavolo nero

**Instructions:**

Preheat the oven to 400 degrees.

In a roasting pan, add in the can of drained chickpeas, banana slices and chopped red onion. Toss well to mix.

Season with the powdered curry and coriander seeds.

Place into the oven to roast for 15 minutes or until caramelized.

Tear the cavolo nero into small pieces, add into the chickpea mix. Place back into the oven to bake for 3 minutes.

Remove and serve immediately.

## Indian Spiced Tomato Soup

This is a healthy soap recipe you can make whenever you need something light to settle your stomach.

**Ingredient List:**

1 cup of brown rice

2 Tablespoons of butter

1 yellow onion, chopped

1 teaspoon of sea salt

3 teaspoons of powdered curry

1 teaspoon of coriander seeds

1 teaspoon of cumin seeds

½ teaspoons of crushed red pepper flakes

2, 28-ounce cans of tomatoes, crushed

1, 14 ounce can of coconut milk

½ cup of almonds, thinly sliced

½ cup of cilantro leaves, chopped

**Instructions:**

In a pot set over medium to high heat, add in the brown rice. Add in 2 cups of water. Allow to come to a boil. Lower the heat to low and cover. Cook for

45 minutes or until all of the liquid has been evaporated.

In a separate pot set over medium heat, add in the butter. Add in the chopped yellow onion. Cook for 8 to 10 minutes or until soft.

Add in the powdered curry, coriander seeds, cumin seeds, crushed red pepper flakes and dash of sea salt. Stir well to mix. Cook for 1 minute.

Add in the can of crushed tomatoes and 6 cups of water. Allow to come to a boil. Lower the heat to low and cook for 10 minutes.

Pour the soup into a blender. Blend on the highest setting until smooth in consistency. Add in the coconut milk and blend again until mixed. Pour back into the pot and allow to come to a simmer.

In a skillet set over medium heat, add in the sliced almonds. Cook for 2 minutes or until fragrant.

Serve the rice on a plate with a topping of the soup, toasted almonds and chopped cilantro.

# Ginger and Turmeric Rice

This is a dish that can be served as a side dish or a standalone meal. Either way, it is packed with a delicious flavor I know you won't be able to get enough of.

## Ingredient List:

1 cup of basmati brown rice

1 tablespoon of coconut oil

2 cloves of garlic, minced

1 tablespoon of ginger, peeled and grated

1 teaspoon of turmeric, grated

¾ teaspoons of salt

2 cups of boiling water

1 tablespoon of lemon juice

½ cup of dried cranberries

**Ingredients for serving:**

¼ cup of cilantro, chopped

¼ cup of pine nuts

**Instructions:**

Pour the basmati brown rice into a bowl. Cover with water and set aside to soak for 15 minutes. Drain and set aside.

In a pot set over medium to high heat, add in the coconut oil. Add in the minced garlic and grated ginger. Cook for 3 minutes or until fragrant. Add in the drained rice, grated turmeric and dash of salt. Cook for an additional 2 to 3 minutes.

Add in the boiling water. Lower the heat to low and cook for 30 to 35 minutes or until all of the water has been absorbed.

Fluff the rice with a fork.

Add in the lemon juice and dried cranberries. Stir well to mix.

Remove from heat. Serve immediately with the chopped cilantro and pine nuts over the top.

## Hearty American Beef Stew

This is a simple one pot dish you can make whenever you need something easy to make. It is a traditional dish the entire family will fall in love with.

**Ingredient List:**

2 Tablespoons of extra virgin olive oil

1 pound of lean beef stew meat, cut into cubes

2 onions, chopped

4 carrots, cut into cubes

2 cups of leeks, chopped

6 cloves of garlic, chopped

2, 14.5-ounce cans of tomatoes, chopped

2, 6-ounce cans of tomato paste

2, 14.5-ounce cans of low sodium beef broth

3 Tablespoons of dried oregano

2 cups of water

2 potatoes, cut into cubes

1 ¼ pounds of green beans

2 cups of kale, chopped

Dash of salt and black pepper

**Instructions:**

In a stockpot set over medium to high heat, add in the olive oil. Add in the beef cubes. Cook for 5 minutes or until browned. Remove from the stockpot and set aside.

In the same pot, add in the chopped onions. Cook for 5 minutes or until translucent.

Add in the carrots, chopped leeks and minced garlic. Continue to cook for an additional 5 minutes or until soft.

Add the beef back into the stock pot. Add in the tomatoes, cans of tomato paste, low sodium beef broth, dried oregano and water. Allow to come to a boil. Lower the heat to low and cook for 1 hour at a simmer or until the beef is soft.

Add in the potato cubes and allow to come back to a boil. Lower the heat to low and cook for 15 minutes or until the potatoes are soft.

Add in the green beans and chopped kale. Cook for 6 to 8 minutes or until the kale is soft.

Season with a dash of salt and black pepper.

Remove from heat and serve immediately.

# Cauliflower Curry Soup

This is a light and hearty soup recipe that is packed with so much flavor, it will leave you craving it for days to come.

**Ingredient List:**

2 Tablespoons of extra virgin olive oil

2 carrots, chopped

2 stalks of celery, chopped

1 onion, chopped

3 cloves of garlic, minced

2 teaspoons of ginger, minced

1 teaspoon of powdered curry

½ teaspoons of powdered turmeric

1 head of cauliflower, cut into pieces

1 russet potato, cut into pieces

2 carrots, chopped

2 stalks of celery, chopped

6 cups of vegetable stock

Crushed red pepper flakes, for garnish and optional

## Instructions:

In a stock pot set over medium to high heat, add in the olive oil. Add in the chopped carrots, chopped onion, chopped celery, minced garlic, minced ginger, powdered curry and powdered turmeric. Stir well to mix. Cook for 5 minutes or until the onion is soft.

Add in the chopped cauliflower, potato pieces, chopped carrots, chopped stalks of celery and vegetable stock. Stir well to mix.

Allow to come to a boil. Lower the heat to low and cook for 20 to 25 minutes or until the vegetables are soft.

Pour the mixture into a blender. Blend on the highest setting until smooth in consistency.

Pour the mixture back into the pot and allow to come to a simmer.

Remove from heat and serve immediately.

## Lemon and Garlic Spaghetti

Make this delicious and simple dish whenever you need something easy to make in a hurry. It is so easy to make, you can have it ready on your table in just a matter of minutes.

**Ingredient List:**
2 to 3 cups of garlic, chopped
4 cloves of garlic, minced
12 ounces of spaghetti
2 Tablespoons of butter
4 Tablespoons of extra virgin olive oil
1 lemon, juice only
1 lemon, zest only
Dash of salt and black pepper

**Instructions:**

Prepare the pasta according to the directions on the package. Once cooked, drain the pasta and set aside. Be sure to reserved ½ cup of the pasta water. In a skillet set over medium to high heat, add in the olive oil. Add in the minced garlic. Cook for 3 minutes.

Add in the butter and lemon juice. Stir well until the butter is melted.

Add the cooked spaghetti into the skillet. Add in the lemon zest and reserved pasta water. Toss well to mix.

Season with a dash of salt and black pepper.

Remove from heat and serve.

## Spiced Apple and Carrot Muffins

These are the perfect muffins for you to make whenever you are craving something on the sweet side.

## Ingredient List:

1 carrot, grated

1 Fuji apple, peeled and grated

2 eggs, beaten

1/3 cup of coconut milk

3 Tablespoons of maple syrup

1 teaspoon of ginger, peeled and grated

¼ cup of almond meal

¾ cup of brown rice flour

1 tablespoon of baker's style baking powder

1 teaspoon of powdered cinnamon

1/8 teaspoons of powdered nutmeg

¼ teaspoons of salt

## Instructions:

Heat the oven to 375 degrees. Grease a muffin pan with cooking spray.

In a bowl, add in the eggs, milk, pure maple syrup and grated ginger. Stir well to mix. Add in the carrot and grated apple. Stir well again to mix.

In a separate bowl, add in the almond meal, baker's style baking powder, powdered cinnamon, powdered nutmeg and salt. Stir well to mix. Pour into coconut milk. Stir well to evenly incorporated. Pour into the muffin pan, filling the muffin cups ¾ of the way full.

Place into the oven to bake for 20 to 25 minutes or until baked through.

Remove and cool for 10 minutes before serving.

## Black Risotto

This is a simple and flavorful dish that will help increase your appetite. Feel free to top this dish with your favorite toppings for the tastiest results.

### Ingredient List:
1/3 cup of extra virgin olive oil
1 onion, chopped

4 cloves of garlic, grated

3 to 4 Tablespoons of flat leaf parsley, chopped

Dash of salt and black pepper

¼ cup of red wine

¼ cup of red wine vinegar

1 cup of arborio rice

1 clove of garlic, grated

1 tablespoon of extra virgin olive oil

1 onion, chopped

Lemon, sliced

Parsley, chopped and for garnish

**Instructions:**

In a saucepan set over medium to high heat, add in 1/3 cup of olive oil. Add in the onion. Cook for 5 minutes or until soft.

Add in the red wine and red wine vinegar. Continue to cook for an additional 5 minutes.

Season with a dash of salt and black pepper.

Add in the arborio rice and 1 tablespoon of extra virgin olive oil. Cover with water and cover. Allow to come to a boil. Lower the heat to low and cook for 25 minutes or until the liquid has been absorbed. In a separate skillet set over medium heat, add in 1 tablespoon of olive oil. Add in the remaining chopped onion. Cook for 5 minutes or until soft. Add in the grated clove of garlic. Cook for an additional 1 to 2 minutes. Season with a dash of salt. Serve the risotto with a topping of the chopped onion, lemon slices and chopped parsley.

## Moroccan Vegetable and Chickpea Tagine

This is a dish that you can make whenever you are craving something on the exotic side. Packed full of authentic Moroccan flavors, this is a dish everyone in your home will love.

**Ingredient List:**

2 Tablespoons of coconut oil

1 onion, chopped

1 clove of garlic, minced

1 tablespoon of powdered cumin

1 tablespoon of powdered coriander

½ Tablespoons of smoked paprika

1 tablespoon of powdered cinnamon

½ teaspoons of sumac

Dash of powdered chili

1 tablespoon of ginger root

2 carrots, chopped

1 sweet potato, skin on and chopped into cubes

1 aubergine, chopped into cubes

1, 14.5 ounce can of chickpeas, drained

2, 14-ounce cans of tomatoes, chopped

3 cups of water

1 handful of dates, chopped

1 handful of parsley, chopped

**Instructions:**

In a pot set over medium to high heat, add in the coconut oil. Add in the chopped onion and minced garlic. Cook for 5 minutes or until soft.

Add in the powdered cumin, powdered coriander, sumac, smoked paprika, powdered cinnamon, dash of powdered chili and ginger root. Stir well to mix.

Add in 1 ½ to 2 cups of water, the cans of chopped tomatoes, chopped carrots and sweet potato cubes. Stir well to incorporate. Cook for 20 minutes or until the vegetables are soft.

Add in the chopped aubergine cubes. Continue to cook for an additional 10 minutes.

Add in the can of chickpeas, chopped dates and handful of chopped parsley. Stir well to incorporate. Remove and serve immediately.

# Classic Vegetable Soup

Make this delicious soup dish whenever you need something easy on the stomach. It is packed full of vegetables, you won't need to eat vegetables for the rest of the day.

## Ingredient List:

32-ounce container of vegetable broth

4-ounce cans of tomato paste

1 potato, chopped

1 carrot, chopped

½ of an onion, chopped

½ cup of frozen peas

½ cup of frozen corn

1 cup of string beans, chopped

½ of a clove of garlic, minced

1 to 2 cups of kale, chopped

Dash of salt and black pepper

## Instructions:

In a saucepan set over medium to high heat, add in all of the ingredients except for the kale. Stir well to mix.

Allow to come to a boil. Cover and lower the heat to low.

Cook for 30 minutes or until the vegetables are soft.

Add in the kale. Cook for 5 minutes or until wilted.

## Quinoa Cakes

Quinoa is known worldwide for its beneficial qualities. It is a light yet healthy snack that is perfect to enjoy any time of the day.

## Ingredient List:

2 ½ cups of quinoa, cooked and chilled

2 eggs

½ cup of red bell pepper, chopped

½ cup of red cabbage, shredded

½ cup of kale, shredded

2 cloves of garlic, minced

1 carrot, chopped

2 stalks of scallions, chopped

1 teaspoon of powdered cumin

4 basil leaves

½ bunch of cilantro, chopped

2 teaspoons of powdered turmeric

¼ cup of tofu

½ Tablespoons of low sodium soy sauce

2/3 cup of Jarlsberg cheese, shredded

Extra virgin olive oil, as needed

**Instructions:**

In a bowl, add in the cooked quinoa and shredded Jarlsberg cheese. Stir well to mix. Set aside.

In a food processor, add in the remaining ingredients. Pulse until well incorporated. Transfer into the bowl with the quinoa. Stir well to mix.

In a skillet set over medium to high heat, add in 1 teaspoon of olive oil. Scoop in 1/3 cup of the mix into the skillet and shape into patties. Cook for 5 minutes on each side or until browned. Repeat. Serve immediately.

## Yogurt Protein Shake

A refreshing, high-protein shake loaded with vitamins, minerals, and fiber, great for breakfast or anytime. Using frozen fruit will make the drink thick, almost like an ice cream shake. Try this with any of your favorite berries.

### Ingredients

½ cup nonfat or low-fat Greek yogurt 1½ teaspoons protein powder (made with whey, soy, or egg)

½ cup chopped fresh or frozen fruit, such as cherries, berries, peaches, or melon

1 banana, sliced

¼ cup or more fruit juice

1 or 2 pitted dates (optional)

## Instructions

Combine all the ingredients in a blender, mixing until smooth. Add more fruit juice, if necessary, to reach the desired consistency.

## Variation: Strawberry Shake

½ cup nonfat or low-fat strawberry Greek yogurt

½ cup frozen strawberries

½ cup apple juice

1 banana, sliced

1½ teaspoons protein powder

2 pitted dates (optional)

## Instructions

Combine all the ingredients in a blender, mixing until smooth. Add more fruit juice, if necessary, to reach the desired consistency.

## Cooking Tip

For variety, substitute vanilla-flavored soy milk for the yogurt or fruit juice. Add 2 ounces silken tofu for extra protein, carbohydrates, and fiber. Toss in about a dozen almonds for extra protein and calories.

## Great Grains Breakfast Cereal

Cooked whole grains are a good way to start your day. Add two or three tablespoons of chopped nuts to the cooked cereal, or swirl in a tablespoon of nut butter for added protein. For a breakfast express meal, make this cereal the night before and warm it up in the morning.

## Ingredients

4 cups water

1 cup whole oats, buckwheat groats, or cornmeal

1 teaspoon vanilla extract

Seasonal fruit (berries, apples, pears, or other fruit), chopped

Soy milk, cow's milk, or nut milk

¼ cup nuts (such as almonds or walnuts), finely chopped

## Instructions

In a medium saucepan, bring the water to a boil over medium heat. Add the grains and vanilla. Cook until the grains are tender but still well defined, 10 to 15 minutes.

Remove from the heat, stir in the chopped fruit, and flavor with the milk. Spoon into bowls and top each serving with 1 tablespoon chopped nuts.

## Apple Muesli

Muesli is a great comfort food that is easily digested and provides sustained energy. Fresh peaches, nectarines, or berries may be served alongside.

### Ingredients

1½ cups old-fashioned rolled oats

1½ cups nonfat or low-fat milk

1½ tablespoons freshly squeezed lemon juice

2 Granny Smith or Fuji apples, cored and grated

¼ cup nuts (such as almonds or walnuts), finely chopped

1 tablespoon raisins

½ teaspoon ground cinnamon

## Instructions

Combine the oats and milk in a large bowl. Let stand for 15 minutes.

In a small bowl, sprinkle the lemon juice over the grated apple, then drain.

Stir the apple into the oat mixture. Spoon into bowls and sprinkle with the nuts, raisins, and cinnamon.

## Whole Grain Pancakes

These fiber-rich, versatile pancakes are a wonderful addition to your breakfast repertoire. This batter also makes great waffles—just reduce the milk to 1¼ cups.

### Ingredients

2 cups whole wheat pastry flour

1 tablespoon baking powder

½ teaspoon kosher salt

1 tablespoon brown sugar, date sugar, or fruit juice concentrate

3 large eggs, separated, or 2 egg whites and 2 whole eggs, separated

2 cups nonfat buttermilk or soy milk

1 tablespoon butter or no-trans-fat margarine, melted

**Instructions**

Heat a lightly greased frying pan over medium-high heat.

Sift together the flour, baking powder, and salt in a medium bowl. Set aside.

In a large mixing bowl, beat together the sweetener, egg yolks, buttermilk, and melted butter. Mix in the dry ingredients until just moist.

In a separate bowl, beat the egg whites to stiff peaks and gently fold them into the batter.

Using a ¼-cup measure, drop the batter onto the hot frying pan, spacing the pancakes at least 2 inches apart. Cook until golden brown on each side.

## Cooking Tip

For variety, try using other whole grains such as oat bran, oat flour, amaranth flour, cornmeal, rolled oats, or buckwheat flour. Consider adding chopped fruit, nuts, or sunflower seeds to the batter.

## Breakfast Burritos

Breakfast burritos scrambled eggs and beans wrapped in a tortilla and topped with salsa, sour cream, or plain yogurt are a popular breakfast item at fast-food restaurants. Simple to make and delicious, this recipe provides a healthy alternative.

## Ingredients

2 teaspoons extra-virgin olive oil

½ cup chopped onion

½ green or red bell pepper, chopped

2 cloves garlic, minced

½ teaspoon ground cumin

4 large eggs, beaten (or use 3 egg whites and 1 whole egg)

One 15-ounce can nonfat refried beans

4 whole wheat tortillas

½ cup plain nonfat yogurt or low-fat sour cream

Salsa

## Instructions

Preheat the oven to 350 degrees F.

In a large skillet, heat the oil over medium heat. Add the onion, bell pepper, and garlic. Sauté until tender. Add the cumin and remove from the heat.

Pour the beaten eggs over the vegetables. Return the skillet to medium heat and carefully stir until the eggs are soft and well scrambled.

Warm the beans in a small saucepan.

Wrap the tortillas in aluminum foil and warm them in the oven for about 10 minutes.

Fill each tortilla with a quarter of the eggs and beans. Top with yogurt or sour cream. Add salsa to taste. Roll up the tortillas, folding in the ends to form burritos. Serve immediately.

## Banana Bran Muffins

Most muffins are high in sugars and fat not these fruit- and fiber-rich treats.

### Ingredients

½ cup whole wheat pastry flour

½ cup unbleached all-purpose flour

¼ cup sugar

2½ teaspoons baking powder

½ teaspoon kosher salt

1 cup wheat bran

1 large egg, well beaten

1 ripe banana, mashed

¼ cup nonfat or low-fat milk

2 tablespoons canola oil

1½ teaspoons ground cinnamon

1 teaspoon vanilla extract

**Instructions**

Preheat the oven to 400 degrees F. Spray 10 muffin cups with nonstick cooking spray or line with paper baking cups.

In a large mixing bowl, sift together the whole wheat and all-purpose flours, sugar, baking powder, and salt. Stir in the bran.

Add the egg, banana, milk, oil, cinnamon, and vanilla and stir until just moist.

Pour the batter into the prepared muffin pan, filling each cup halfway.

Bake for 20 to 25 minutes, or until the muffins spring back when touched in the center. Remove from the pan and allow to cool.

## Applesauce Muffins

These muffins use only natural sweeteners and make a wonderful breakfast or an easy lunch. Serve with yogurt and fresh fruit.

### Ingredients

½ cup raisins

½ cup unsweetened apple juice concentrate

1 ripe banana, sliced

¼ cup canola oil

1 teaspoon vanilla extract

½ cup unsweetened applesauce

1 large egg

1 cup whole wheat flour

½ cup wheat germ

½ teaspoon baking powder

½ teaspoon baking soda

¼ teaspoon kosher salt

1 tablespoon ground cinnamon

**Instructions**

Preheat the oven to 400 degrees F. Spray a 12-cup muffin pan with nonstick cooking spray or line with paper baking cups.

Heat the raisins and apple juice concentrate in a small saucepan over medium heat until the raisins are soft, about 3 minutes. Pour into a blender and puree.

Add the banana, oil, vanilla, applesauce, and egg to the blender and puree.

In a large mixing bowl, combine the flour, wheat germ, baking powder, baking soda, salt, and cinnamon and stir well.

Add the wet ingredients to the dry ingredients and stir just until moist.

Pour the batter into the prepared muffin tin, filling each cup halfway.

Bake for 20 minutes, or until the muffins spring back when touched in the center. Remove from the pan and allow to cool.

## Oat and Date Scones

Scones are traditionally richer than regular biscuits due to the butter and egg. This recipe balances out that richness by being packed with fiber and whole grains, including oat flour.

## Ingredients

1 cup unbleached all-purpose flour

½ cup whole wheat pastry flour

½ cup oat flour (place oatmeal in a blender and grind for 1 minute or so)

¼ cup brown sugar

2 teaspoons baking powder

½ teaspoon baking soda

½ cup (1 stick) butter or no-trans-fat margarine, cut into pieces

½ cup chopped dates

1 large egg, lightly beaten

½ cup low-fat buttermilk

## Instructions

Preheat the oven to 375 degrees F.

In a large mixing bowl, combine the all-purpose flour, whole wheat flour, oat flour, brown sugar, baking powder, and baking soda.

Using a fork or a pastry cutter, blend in the butter until the mixture is crumbly. Stir in the dates.

Add the egg and buttermilk, stirring with a fork until the dough holds together. Do not overmix.

Gently knead the dough a few times on a lightly floured board. Add up to 2 tablespoons more flour if the dough seems too sticky to work with.

Shape the dough into a flat 8-inch round. Cut into 8 wedges and arrange 2 inches apart on a nonstick baking sheet.

Bake for 20 minutes, or until golden brown. Serve warm.

## Savory Breakfast Strata with Swiss Chard and Gruyère

This savory dish of baked eggs combined with whole wheat bread cubes, Swiss chard, and Gruyère is a brunch hit. Serve any leftovers with our Spinach

Salad with Poppy Seed Balsamic Vinaigrette, for a satisfying lunch. Note that this recipe requires at least an hour to prepare, and another hour for baking.

**Ingredients**

½ loaf (½ pound) whole wheat french bread, cut into 1-inch cubes (about 6 cups), divided

½ bunch rainbow chard or Swiss chard

1 tablespoon extra-virgin olive oil

1 clove garlic, minced

½ pound cremini mushrooms, chopped (about 2 cups)

½ cup (about 2 ounces) shredded Gruyère or Swiss cheese

6 large eggs

¾ cup milk

⅛ teaspoon freshly ground black pepper

## Ingredients

Spray an 8-inch square baking dish with nonstick cooking spray. Layer half of the bread cubes in the bottom of the dish until it is fully covered.

Wash the chard and pat dry. Remove the stems and chop into ½-inch pieces. Cut the leaves into 2-inch pieces. You should have about 4 cups of chopped chard.

In a large frying pan, heat the oil over medium heat, and add the chopped chard stems. Cook for 2 minutes, or until tender. Add the chard leaves and garlic and cook for another 3 to 4 minutes, or until the leaves are wilted. Layer the chard over the bread cubes in the baking dish.

Put the mushrooms in the same frying pan and sauté for about 5 minutes, or until lightly browned and soft.

Layer the mushrooms over the chard, and then sprinkle with the shredded cheese. Layer the remaining bread cubes over the top.

In a large bowl, beat the eggs and milk with a fork. Add the pepper, and then pour the mixture evenly over the bread cubes.

Cover the dish and refrigerate for at least 1 hour or preferably overnight.

Preheat the oven to 375 degrees F.

Bake the strata, uncovered, for 55 to 60 minutes, or until a knife inserted 1 inch from the center comes out clean. Remove from oven and let stand for 5 minutes before serving.

## Papaya, Shrimp, and Spinach Salad with Lime Vinaigrette

An easy-to-prepare salad, this dish has a medley of colors and flavors.

## Ingredients

1 head butter lettuce

1 bunch fresh spinach

1 large, firm-ripe papaya, peeled, seeded, and diced

1 large orange, peeled and diced

1 large, ripe avocado, peeled, pitted, and diced

½ cup sliced almonds, lightly toasted

½ pound cooked bay shrimp (optional)

½ cup Lime Vinaigrette (recipe follows)

## Instructions

Wash and dry the lettuce and spinach, and cut or tear into bite-size pieces. Place in a large bowl and add the diced papaya, orange, avocado, almonds, and shrimp.

Drizzle in some of the Lime Vinaigrette and toss gently to coat the salad evenly.

Serve immediately, passing the remaining vinaigrette at the table.

# Lime Vinaigrette

## Ingredients

¼ cup lime marmalade (preferably Rose's)

Juice of 2 medium limes (about ¼ cup)

2 teaspoons orange juice concentrate

½ teaspoon Dijon mustard

½ teaspoon kosher salt

½ teaspoon ground coriander

⅛ teaspoon cayenne pepper

⅓ cup canola oil

## Instructions

Place the lime marmalade in a medium bowl and stir until the lumps are dissolved.

Add the lime juice and whisk until smooth. Stir in the orange juice concentrate, mustard, salt, coriander, and cayenne.

Slowly whisk in the oil until the dressing is smooth and emulsified.

## Crunchy Broccoli and Carrot Salad

This bold, crunchy salad is tangy-sweet with vibrant colors and flavors. Leftovers will keep well for several days to provide handy lunches or snacks.

### Ingredients

3 broccoli crowns with stems

1½ cups shredded carrots

4 green onions, sliced

½ cup raisins

¼ cup dried cranberries

¼ cup low-fat mayonnaise

⅓ cup rice vinegar

¼ teaspoon freshly ground black pepper

## Instructions

Break the broccoli crowns into florets and cut the stems into ½-inch or smaller pieces (if they are too large, they won't absorb the dressing well). You should have about 6 cups chopped broccoli.

Put the broccoli, carrots, green onions, raisins, and cranberries in a large bowl and mix well.

Whisk the mayonnaise, rice vinegar, and pepper in a small bowl. Pour the dressing over the broccoli mixture and toss to coat.

Let the salad stand for at least 30 minutes, or overnight, before serving. Store any leftover salad in a resealable container in the refrigerator for several days.

# Spinach Salad with Poppy Seed Balsamic Vinaigrette

A special dressing makes this spinach salad stand out from the crowd. In spring and summer, add fresh strawberries. In autumn and winter, try dried apricots.

## Ingredients

1 tablespoon poppy seeds

1 tablespoon sesame seeds

2 tablespoons sugar

¼ cup balsamic vinegar

2 tablespoons extra-virgin olive oil

3 tablespoons grape or apple juice (grape adds a nice flavor)

½ teaspoon Worcestershire sauce

½ teaspoon paprika

2 bunches spinach

½ cup walnuts or hazelnuts, chopped

2 tablespoons chopped green onion, for garnish (optional)

## Instructions

To make the poppy seed dressing, in a small bowl, whisk together the poppy and sesame seeds, sugar, balsamic vinegar, oil, juice, Worcestershire, and paprika.

To assemble the salad, wash the spinach and tear it into bite-size pieces (you should have about 4 cups). Put into a large salad bowl. Pour the vinaigrette over the spinach. Toss the salad and top with the nuts and green onion.

## Avocado-Dressed Fresh Kale Salad

Enjoy the vital flavors of raw kale paired with sweet corn and avocado. Use in-season corn if possible as it's sweeter and has a nice texture, though frozen corn will work too. Prepared with the help of a food processor, this recipe is grown-up food that's fun to make—you'll be getting your hands dirty with this one.

**Ingredients**

1 bunch fresh dill

1 red or sweet onion

2 cloves garlic

1 bunch raw kale (any variety)

1 red bell pepper, seeded and diced (about 1 cup)

1 large or 2 small roma tomatoes, diced (about 1 cup)

Kernels from 2 to 3 ears corn, or 2 to 3 cups thawed frozen corn

Juice of 1 lemon (about 3 tablespoons)

3 tablespoons balsamic vinegar

2 tablespoons extra-virgin olive oil

1 to 2 medium ripe avocados

## Instructions

Pulse the dill in a food processor until finely chopped, then transfer to a large bowl. Pulse the onion and garlic until finely chopped and transfer to the bowl. Pulse the kale, in 2 or 3 batches as needed, until finely chopped and transfer to the bowl.

Add the bell pepper, tomato, and corn to the bowl. In a small bowl, whisk together the lemon juice, balsamic vinegar, and oil. Pour over the vegetables and toss.

Scoop the avocados into the bowl. Using clean hands, mash all the ingredients together. The avocados should be "absorbed" into the salad.

Cover and refrigerate for at least 1 hour, or overnight, before serving. The salad keeps well for 3 to 4 days in the refrigerator.

# Texas Black Bean Salad

Rich black beans, crunchy corn, and a hint of chili make this a perfect dinner or side dish. Make a large batch and freeze extra servings for later.

## Ingredients

Two 15-ounce cans low-sodium black beans (about 3 cups), drained

1 cup diced sweet onion (½ medium onion)

1 cup diced red bell pepper (½ large pepper)

1 cup diced green bell pepper (½ large pepper)

2 cups fresh or thawed frozen organic corn

¼ cup chopped fresh cilantro or parsley

Juice from 2 limes (about ¼ cup)

2 tablespoons extra-virgin olive oil

1½ to 2 teaspoons chili powder

½ to 1 teaspoon ground cumin

½ teaspoon dried oregano

Dash of cayenne pepper

Freshly ground black pepper

## Instructions

Put the black beans, onion, red and green peppers, corn, and cilantro in a large bowl and mix well.

In a small bowl, whisk together the lime juice, oil, chili powder, cumin, oregano, cayenne, and black pepper.

Pour the dressing over the bean salad and stir well.

Refrigerate for at least 2 hours before serving.

## Crispy Mock Chicken Salad

With a hint of curry and the sweetness of raisins, this tasty spread can be a topping for mixed greens or stuffed inside a whole wheat pita.

## Ingredients

2 tablespoons canola or coconut oil

One 8-ounce package tempeh, crumbled

1 cup chopped celery

½ cup chopped carrot

½ cup minced fresh parsley

2 tablespoons finely diced red or yellow onion

½ cup low-fat mayonnaise

¼ cup raw cashews

1 tablespoon currants or raisins

1 teaspoon curry powder

Kosher salt and freshly ground black pepper

## Instructions

Heat the oil in a large heavy pan over medium-high heat. Add the crumbled tempeh to the pan and cook for 3 to 4 minutes, or until crispy and golden brown.

Transfer the tempeh to a large bowl and stir in the remaining ingredients. Season to taste with salt and pepper.

# Waldorf Salad

Enjoy the delightful combination of textures in this healthy update of the classic salad.

## Ingredients

¾ cup plain nonfat yogurt

¼ cup low-fat sour cream

¼ cup low-fat mayonnaise

Juice from 1 medium orange (about ¼ cup)

¼ teaspoon ground nutmeg

2 Red or Golden Delicious apples, cored and chopped

2 Fuji or Granny Smith apples, cored and chopped

2 stalks celery, chopped

½ cup walnuts, chopped

½ cup raisins

4 to 6 cups salad greens

## Instructions

To make the dressing, in a small bowl, whisk together the yogurt, sour cream, mayonnaise, orange juice, and nutmeg.

To assemble the salad, in a medium bowl, combine the apples, celery, grapes, walnuts, and raisins.

Toss the dressing with the apple mixture. Chill.

Serve the salad on a bed of greens.

# Conclusion

Cancer is not contagious like flu or chickenpox. You cannot catch cancer from someone who has it.

Many cancers develop because of lifestyle habits such as smoking, excessive drinking of alcohol or eating too much fat (especially animal fat). Others are caused by factors in the environment such as sunlight, radiation and some industrial chemicals. By leading a healthy lifestyle and avoiding certain risk factors, about one third of all cancers can be prevented from occurring.

Many people are afraid of cancer because they think it is a death sentence, but when cancer is detected early, treatment is at its most effective. Recognising the early warning signs and going for regular check-ups can save your life.

Speak to your doctor about your personal and family medical history. Certain medical conditions may increase your risk of developing some cancers. For example, people who are carriers of the Hepatitis B virus are more likely to develop liver cancer. Women infected with certain sexually-transmitted infections have a higher chance of getting cervical cancer.

Your doctor can advise you on how to prevent such conditions. But if you already have them, he can tell you what steps you can take to reduce your risk of developing cancer.

Some cancers (like breast and colorectal cancers) tend to run in families. If your parents, brothers or sisters have had cancer, discuss it with your doctor.

He may recommend some screening tests to help determine your risk for developing the same cancer.

The keto diet is designed to increase the body's production of ketones, and force the body to burn fat for energy instead of sugar. Because they are familiar with the chemical action of ketones, scientists are asking if the power of these "mechanisms" could be used to prevent cancer. They also are researching how a keto diet might be used in cancer care to deliver better outcomes.

Printed in Great Britain
by Amazon

25081514R00119